Addressing Base Erosion and Profit Shifting

OECD
BETTER POLICIES FOR BETTER LIVES

Please cite this publication as:
OECD (2013), *Addressing Base Erosion and Profit Shifting*, OECD Publishing.
http://dx.doi.org/10.1787/9789264192744-en

ISBN 978-92-64-19265-2 (print)
ISBN 978-92-64-19274-4 (PDF)

Photo credit: Cover © John Gollop / iStockPhoto.

Corrigenda to OECD publications may be found on line at: *www.oecd.org/publishing/corrigenda*.

Table of contents

Figures

Table

Boxes

Executive summary

Base erosion constitutes a serious risk to tax revenues, tax sovereignty and tax fairness for OECD member countries and non-members alike. While there are many ways in which domestic tax bases can be eroded, a significant source of base erosion is profit shifting. Whilst further work on the data related to base erosion and profit shifting (BEPS) is important and necessary, there is no question that BEPS is a pressing and current issue for a number of jurisdictions. In this context, the G20 has welcomed the work that the OECD is undertaking in this area and has requested a report about progress of the work for their February 2013 meeting.

While there clearly is a tax compliance aspect, as shown by a number of high profile cases, there is a more fundamental policy issue: the international common principles drawn from national experiences to share tax jurisdiction may not have kept pace with the changing business environment. Domestic rules for international taxation and internationally agreed standards are still grounded in an economic environment characterised by a lower degree of economic integration across borders, rather than today's environment of global taxpayers, characterised by the increasing importance of intellectual property as a value-driver and by constant developments of information and communication technologies.

Early on it was recognised that the interaction of domestic tax systems can lead to overlaps in the exercise of taxing rights that can result in double taxation. Domestic and international rules to address double taxation, many of which originated with principles developed by the League of Nations in the 1920s, aim at addressing these overlaps so as to minimise trade distortions and impediments to sustainable economic growth. The interaction of domestic tax systems (including rules adopted in accordance with international standards to relieve double taxation), however, can also lead to gaps that provide opportunities to eliminate or significantly reduce taxation on income in a manner that is inconsistent with the policy objectives of such domestic tax rules and international standards. While multinational corporations urge co-operation in the development of international standards to alleviate double taxation resulting from differences in domestic tax rules, they often exploit differences in domestic tax rules and international standards that provide opportunities to eliminate or significantly reduce taxation.

This report aims to present the issues related to BEPS in an objective and comprehensive manner. The report first describes studies and data available in the public domain regarding the existence and magnitude of BEPS (summaries of the studies are included in Annex B). It then contains an overview of global developments that have an impact on corporate tax matters. The core of the report sets out an overview of the key principles that underlie the taxation of cross-border activities, as well as the BEPS opportunities these principles may create. It also analyses some well-known corporate structures (described in more detail in Annex C) and highlights the most important issues that these structures raise.

The report concludes that, in addition to a need for increased transparency on effective tax rates of MNEs, key pressure areas include those related to:

- International mismatches in entity and instrument characterisation including, hybrid mismatch arrangements and arbitrage;
- Application of treaty concepts to profits derived from the delivery of digital goods and services;
- The tax treatment of related party debt-financing, captive insurance and other intra-group financial transactions;
- Transfer pricing, in particular in relation to the shifting of risks and intangibles, the artificial splitting of ownership of assets between legal entities within a group, and transactions between such entities that would rarely take place between independents;
- The effectiveness of anti-avoidance measures, in particular GAARs, CFC regimes, thin capitalisation rules and rules to prevent tax treaty abuse;
- The availability of harmful preferential regimes.

A number of indicators show that the tax practices of some multinational companies have become more aggressive over time, raising serious compliance and fairness issues. These issues were already flagged by tax commissioners at the 2006 meeting of the Forum on Tax Administration in Seoul and different instruments have been developed to better analyse and react to aggressive tax planning schemes which result in massive revenue losses. The OECD work on aggressive tax planning, including its directory of aggressive tax planning schemes, is being used by government officials from several countries. Some countries are intensively drawing on this work to improve their audit performance. Improving tax compliance, on-shore and off-shore, remains a key priority for both securing governments' revenue and levelling the playing field for businesses. It requires determined action from tax administrations, which should co-operate in exchanging intelligence and information, as well as monitoring the effectiveness of the strategies used, for example in terms of additional tax revenue assessed/collected, and in terms of enhanced compliance.

This report also shows that current international tax standards may not have kept pace with changes in global business practices, in particular in the area of intangibles and the development of the digital economy. For example, today it is possible to be heavily involved in the economic life of another country, *e.g.* by doing business with customers located in that country via the internet, without having a taxable presence there or in another country that levies tax on profits. In an era where non-resident taxpayers can derive substantial profits from transacting with customers located in another country, questions are being raised on whether the current rules are fit for purpose. Further, as businesses increasingly integrate across borders and tax rules often remain unco-ordinated, there are a number of structures, technically legal, which take advantage of asymmetries in domestic and international tax rules.

The OECD has already produced analytical work to better understand and react to the issue of hybrid mismatch arrangements through which taxable income in effect disappears (*Hybrid Mismatch Arrangements: Policy and Compliance Issues,* 2012). Work has also been launched to address some of the new challenges. Proposals to update the OECD's transfer pricing guidelines in the area of intangibles and to simplify their application have been tabled and should be advanced quickly to provide immediate responses to some of the most critical profit shifting challenges. Simplification should also ensure that tax administrations have access to better tools for assessing tax compliance risks. This involves the development of documentation requirements able to provide tax auditors with the full picture of business operations. In the recent past, the OECD also identified a number of avenues to better assess tax compliance risks, such as those described in *Tackling Aggressive Tax Planning through Improved Transparency and Disclosure* (OECD, 2011). Finally, major progress towards transparency has been achieved over the past four years with the establishment of the Global Forum on Transparency and Exchange of Information for Tax Purposes.

More fundamentally, a holistic approach is necessary to properly address the issue of BEPS. Government actions should be comprehensive and deal with all the different aspects of the issue. These include, for example, the balance between source and residence taxation, the tax treatment of intra-group financial transactions, the implementation of anti-abuse provisions, including CFC legislation, as well as transfer pricing rules. A comprehensive approach, globally supported, should draw on an in-depth analysis of the interaction of all these pressure points. It is clear that co-ordination will be key in the implementation of any solution, though countries may not all use the same instruments to address the issue of BEPS.

What is at stake is the integrity of the corporate income tax. A lack of response would further undermine competition, as some businesses, such as those which operate cross-border and have access to sophisticated tax expertise, may profit from BEPS opportunities and therefore have unintended competitive advantages compared with enterprises that operate mostly at the domestic level. In addition to issues of fairness, this may lead to an inefficient allocation of resources by distorting investment decisions towards activities that have lower pre-tax rates of return, but higher after-tax rates of return. Finally, if other taxpayers (including ordinary individuals) think that multinational corporations can legally avoid paying income tax it will undermine voluntary compliance by all taxpayers – upon which modern tax administration depends.

Because many BEPS strategies take advantage of the interface between the tax rules of different countries, it may be difficult for any single country, acting alone, to fully address the issue. Furthermore unilateral and uncoordinated actions by governments responding in isolation could result in the risk of double – and possibly multiple – taxation for business. This would have a negative impact on investment, and thus on growth and employment globally. In this context, the major challenge is not only to identify appropriate responses, but also the mechanisms to implement them in a streamlined manner, in spite of the well-known existing legal constraints, such as the existence of more than 3 000 bilateral tax treaties. It is therefore essential that countries consider innovative approaches to implement comprehensive solutions.

Developing a global action plan to address beps

A comprehensive action plan

In order to address base erosion and profit shifting, which is fundamentally due to a large number of interacting factors, a comprehensive action plan should be developed quickly. The main purpose of that plan would be to provide countries with instruments, domestic and international, aiming at better aligning rights to tax with real economic activity.

While it is useful to take stock of the work which has already been done and which is underway, it is also important to revisit some of the fundamentals of the existing standards. Indeed, incremental approaches may help curb the current trends but will not respond to several of the challenges governments face.

Though governments may have to provide unilateral solutions, there is value and necessity in providing an internationally co-ordinated approach. Collaboration and co-ordination will not only facilitate and reinforce domestic actions to protect tax bases, but will also be key to provide comprehensive international solutions that may satisfactorily respond to the issue. Co-ordination in that respect will also limit the need for individual jurisdictions' unilateral tax measures. Of course, jurisdictions may also provide more stringent unilateral actions to prevent BEPS than those in the co-ordinated approach.

The OECD is committed to delivering a global and comprehensive action plan based on in-depth analysis of the identified pressure areas with a view to provide concrete solutions to realign international standards with the current global business environment. This will require some "out of the box" thinking as well as ambition and pragmatism to overcome implementation difficulties, such as the existence of current tax treaties. In the meanwhile, current work will naturally be speeded up where relevant to BEPS.

Timely developed in consultation with all stakeholders

A comprehensive solution cannot be developed without the contribution of all stakeholders. All interested member countries will have to be involved in the development of the action plan and non-member countries, in particular G20 economies, will have to contribute as well. Consultation with the business community, as well as civil society, should be organised so that the views of practitioners and other stakeholders can be taken into account and to provide businesses with the certainty they need to make long-term investment decisions.

There is an urgent need to deal with this issue and the OECD is committed to provide an innovative and timely response to it. It is proposed that an initial comprehensive action plan be developed within the next six months so that the Committee on Fiscal Affairs can agree it at its next meeting in June 2013. Such an action plan should *(i)* identify actions needed to address BEPS, *(ii)* set deadlines to implement these actions and *(iii)* identify the resources needed and the methodology to implement these actions.

To develop such a plan, the CFA has given a mandate to the CFA Bureau together with the chairs of the relevant working groups, to work with the OECD Secretariat, in consultation with interested countries and other stakeholders. The CFA Bureau and the chairs of the working parties will call on available expertise through a series of physical or virtual meetings and will monitor the work so that a draft action plan can be submitted to the CFA in time for it to be discussed and approved at its June 2013 meeting.

Focusing on the main pressure areas

On substance, the development of the action plan should provide a comprehensive response that takes into account the links between the different pressure areas. Moreover, better information and data on BEPS will be sought.

The different components of the action plan will include proposals to develop:

- Instruments to put an end to or neutralise the effects of hybrid mismatch arrangements and arbitrage.
- Improvements or clarifications to transfer pricing rules to address specific areas where the current rules produce undesirable results from a policy perspective. The current work on intangibles, which is a particular area of concern, would be included in a broader reflection on transfer pricing rules.
- Updated solutions to the issues related to jurisdiction to tax, in particular in the areas of digital goods and services. These solutions may include a revision of treaty provisions.
- More effective anti-avoidance measures, as a complement to the previous items. Anti-avoidance measures can be included in domestic laws or included in international instruments. Examples of these measures include General Anti-Avoidance Rules, Controlled Foreign Companies rules, Limitation of benefits rules and other anti-treaty abuse provisions.
- Rules on the treatment of intra-group financial transactions, such as those related to the deductibility of payments and the application of withholding taxes.
- Solutions to counter harmful regimes more effectively, taking into account factors such as transparency and substance.

The action plan will also consider the best way to implement in a timely fashion the measures governments can agree upon. If treaty changes are required, solutions for a quick implementation of these changes should be examined and proposed as well. OECD has developed standards to eliminate double taxation and should ensure that this goal is achieved while efforts are deployed to also prevent double non-taxation. In this respect, a comprehensive approach should also consider possible improvements to eliminate double taxation, such as increased efficiency of mutual agreement procedures and arbitration provisions.

Immediate action from our tax administrations is also needed

The Forum on Tax Administration gathers the Tax Commissioners of all OECD and G20 countries. The Forum will meet in Moscow in May 2013. It is expected that the Tax Commissioners will focus on and communicate on their actions to improve tax compliance, which is a pre-requisite for a fair tax environment. They are invited in particular to draw on the work developed by the OECD in the area of aggressive tax planning, with more than 400 schemes included in the aggressive tax planning directory.

Finally, it is recommended that this report be shared with the G20 in response to their call in November 2012 in Mexico for a report at their next meeting in February in Moscow.

Chapter 1

Introduction

There is a growing perception that governments lose substantial corporate tax revenue because of planning aimed at shifting profits in ways that erode the taxable base to locations where they are subject to a more favourable tax treatment. Recent news stories such as Bloomberg's "The Great Corporate Tax Dodge", the New York Times' "But Nobody Pays That", The Times' "Secrets of Tax Avoiders" and the Guardian's "Tax Gap" are only some examples of the increased attention mainstream media has been paying to corporate tax affairs. Civil society and non-governmental organisations (NGOs) have also been vocal in this respect, sometimes addressing very complex tax issues in a simplistic manner and pointing fingers at transfer pricing rules based on the arm's length principle as the cause of these problems.

This increased attention and the inherent challenge of dealing comprehensively with such a complex subject has encouraged a perception that the domestic and international rules on the taxation of cross-border profits are now broken and that taxes are only paid by the naive. Multinational enterprises (MNEs) are being accused of dodging taxes worldwide, and in particular in developing countries, where tax revenue is critical to foster long-term development.

Business leaders often argue that they have a responsibility towards their shareholders to legally reduce the taxes their companies pay. Some of them might consider most of the accusations unjustified, in some cases deeming governments responsible for incoherent tax policies and for designing tax systems that provide incentives for Base Erosion and Profit Shifting (BEPS). They also point out that MNEs are still sometimes faced with double taxation on their profits from cross-border activities, with mutual agreement procedures sometimes unable to resolve disputes among governments in a timely manner or at all.

The debate over BEPS has also reached the political level and has become an issue on the agenda of several OECD and non-OECD countries. The G20 leaders meeting in Mexico on 18-19 June 2012 explicitly referred to "the need to prevent base erosion and profit shifting" in their final Declaration. This message was reiterated at the G20 finance ministers meeting of 5-6 November 2012, the final communiqué of which states: "We also welcome the work that the OECD is undertaking into the problem of base erosion and profit shifting and look forward to a report about progress of the work at our next meeting".

On the margins of the G20 meeting in November 2012, the United Kingdom's Chancellor of the Exchequer, George Osborne, and Germany's Minister of Finance, Wolfgang Schäuble, issued a joint statement, which has since then been joined by France's Economy and Finance Minister, Pierre Moscovici, calling for co-ordinated action to strengthen international tax standards and urging their counterparts to back efforts by the OECD to identify possible gaps in tax laws. Such a concern was also voiced by US President Obama in the *President's Framework for Business Tax Reform*, which states that "empirical evidence suggests that income-shifting behaviour by multinational corporations is a significant concern that should be addressed through tax reform". BEPS is also related to the OECD-wide reflection on "New Approaches to Economic Challenges", whose aim is to respond to the call by several countries for such a reflection, to learn the lessons from the crisis and derive its policy implications, and to build a more solid path for economic growth and well-being.[1]

This report aims at presenting the issues related to BEPS in an objective and comprehensive manner. The report first describes studies and data available in the public domain regarding the existence and magnitude of BEPS (summaries of the studies are included in Annex B). It then contains an overview of global developments that impact on corporate tax matters. The core of the report sets out an overview of the key principles that underlie the taxation of cross-border activities, as well as the BEPS opportunities these principles may create. It also analyses some well-known corporate structures (described in more detail in Annex C) and highlights the most important issues that these structures raise.

Note

1 *http://www.oecd.org/about/secretary-general/newapproachestoeconomicchallengesanoecdagendaforgrowth.htm.*

Chapter 2

How big a problem is BEPS? An overview of the available data

This chapter reproduces data on corporate tax receipts over time, provides an overview of statistics on foreign direct investments, and analyses relevant studies regarding the existence and magnitude of BEPS. It concludes that with the data currently available, it is difficult to reach solid conclusions about how much BEPS actually occurs. Most of the writing on the topic is inconclusive, although there is abundant circumstantial evidence that BEPS behaviours are widespread. There are several studies and data indicating that there is increased segregation between the location where actual business activities and investment take place and the location where profits are reported for tax purposes.

Data on corporate income tax revenues

Across the OECD, corporate income tax raises, on average, revenues equivalent to around 3% of GDP or about 10% of total tax revenues. Although their relative importance varies from country to country, corporate income tax receipts constitute an important component of government revenues. While the scale of revenue losses through BEPS may not be extremely large in relation to tax revenues as a whole, the issue is still relevant in monetary terms and may also be of wider relevance because of its effects on the perceived integrity of the tax system. In terms of trends, the unweighted average of taxes on corporate income as a percentage of total taxation in OECD countries was 8.8% in 1965, dropped to 7.6% in 1975, and then consistently increased over the years until 2007, when the reported average ratio was 10.6%. Starting from 2008, likely due to the economic downturn, the ratio declined to 10% in 2008 and 8.4% in 2009; subsequently it increased to 8.6% in 2010.[1]

The trend towards a reduction of corporate income tax rates started with the tax reforms in the United Kingdom and the United States in the mid-1980s, which broadened the tax base (*e.g.* by making depreciation allowances for tax purposes less generous) and cut statutory rates. Corporation tax rates have continued to be cut in recent years. The statutory corporate income tax rates in OECD member countries dropped on average 7.2 percentage points between 2000 and 2011, from 32.6% to 25.4%. This trend seems to be widespread, as rates have been reduced in 31 countries and increased only in Chile (from 15 to 17%) and Hungary (from 18 to 19%). However, in Hungary a 10% tax rate was also introduced in 2010, up to HUF 500 million (EUR 1.7 million) of the tax base, with the result that the effective tax rate was 14% in 2011.

The cuts in tax rates introduced by these reforms have not led to a fall in the corporate tax burden (measured by the corporate tax-to-GDP ratio). Generally, revenues from corporate income taxes as a share of GDP have increased over time, with the unweighted average of revenues deriving from taxes on corporate income as a percentage of GDP increasing from 2.2% in 1965 to 3.8% in 2007. This positive trend reversed in 2008 and 2009, when the average ratio dropped to 3.5% and 2.8%, respectively. It recovered slightly in 2010, to 2.9%. Figure 2.1 shows the evolution over time of corporate income tax receipts as a percentage of GDP in OECD countries (Annex A contains a country-by-country comparison over the period 1990-2011).

Again, it should be noted that, although they may provide useful indications, these trends in the relationship of corporate income tax to GDP do not necessarily imply either the existence or non-existence of BEPS practices. One reason why corporate tax revenues have been maintained, before the impact of the financial crisis, despite cuts in tax rates, has been base-broadening measures such as aligning depreciation for tax purposes

Figure 2.1. **Taxes on corporate income as a percentage of GDP**

OECD unweighted average

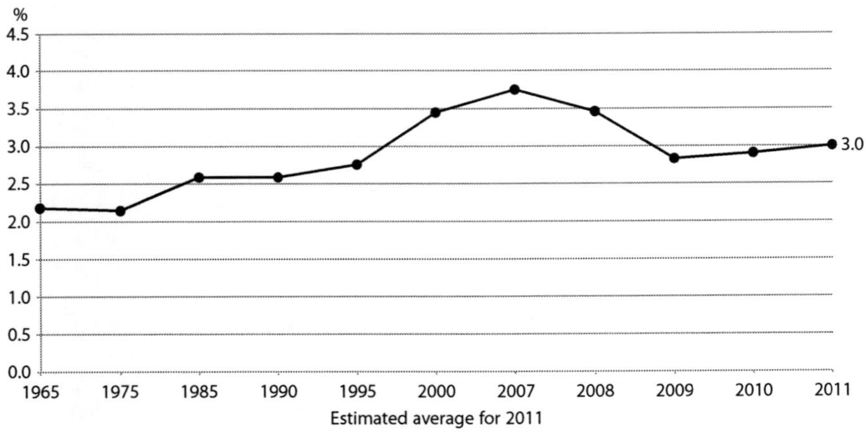

Note: Estimated average for 2011.

Source: OECD (2012), Revenue Statistics 1965-2011.

more closely with actual depreciation, reductions in "tax expenditures" (*i.e.* tax reliefs for particular activities or groups of taxpayers that are in effect equivalent to public expenditure and thus have to be financed through higher taxes elsewhere). Another reason has been an increasing share of corporate income in GDP in many countries, reflecting increased business profits and, in some countries, increased incorporation (*i.e.* more business activity being undertaken in corporate form, with its income being taxed under the corporate income tax). However, further analysis would be required to distinguish the particular factors increasing the corporate income tax base in each country.[2]

Data on Foreign Direct Investments

An analysis of the available data on FDIs may give useful indications in relation to the magnitude of BEPS. Direct investment is a category of cross-border investment made by a resident in one economy (the direct investor) with the objective of establishing a lasting interest in an enterprise (the direct investment enterprise) that is resident in an economy other than that of the direct investor. The motivation of the direct investor is a strategic long-term relationship with the direct investment enterprise to ensure a significant degree of influence by the direct investor in the management of the direct investment enterprise. The "lasting interest" is shown when the direct investor owns at least 10% of the voting power of the direct investment enterprise. Direct investment may also allow the direct investor to gain access to the economy of the direct investment enterprise which it might otherwise be unable to do. The objectives of direct investment are different from those of portfolio investment whereby investors do not generally expect to influence the management of the enterprise.

The OECD and IMF compile statistics on FDIs based on information collected at the national level. More in-depth analyses of these data could be useful. For example, by searching through the IMF Co-ordinated Direct Investment Survey (CDIS), it emerges that in 2010 Barbados, Bermuda and the British Virgin Islands received more FDIs (combined 5.11% of global FDIs) than Germany (4.77%) or Japan (3.76%). During the same year, these three jurisdictions made more investments into the world (combined 4.54%) than Germany (4.28%). On a country-by-country position, in 2010 the British Virgin Islands were the second largest investor into China (14%) after Hong Kong (45%) and before the United States (4%). For the same year, Bermuda appears as the third largest investor in Chile (10%). Similar data exists in relation to other countries, for example Mauritius is the top investor country into India (24%), while Cyprus[3] (28%), the British Virgin Islands (12%), Bermuda (7%) and the Bahamas (6%) are among the top five investors into Russia.

Interesting information may also be gathered from the OECD Investment Database. For certain countries that database breaks down FDI positions (stock)[4] held through so-called special purpose entities (SPEs).[5] In general terms, SPEs are entities with no or few employees, little or no physical presence in the host economy, whose assets and liabilities represent investments in or from other countries, and whose core business consists of group financing or holding activities.[6]

For example, total inward stock investments into the Netherlands for 2011 were equal to USD 3 207 billion. Of this amount, investments through SPEs amounted to USD 2 625 billion. On the other hand, outward stock investments from the Netherlands were equal to USD 4 002 billion, with about USD 3 023 billion being made through SPEs. Similarly, in the case of Luxembourg, total inward stock investments for 2011 were equal to USD 2 129 billion, with USD 1 987 billion being made through SPEs. On the other hand, outward stock investments from Luxembourg were equal to USD 2 140 billion, with about USD 1 945 billion being made through SPEs. The figures are smaller, but still proportionally significant, for two other OECD countries. In the case of Austria total inward stock investments for 2011 were equal to USD 271 billion, with investments through SPE amounting to USD 106 billion. On the other hand, outward stock investments from Austria were equal to USD 300 billion, with about USD 105 billion being made through SPEs. Finally, for Hungary, total inward stock investments for 2011 were equal to USD 233 billion, with investments through SPE amounting to 106 billion USD. On the other hand, outward stock investments were equal to USD 176 billion, with about USD 152 billion being made through SPEs.

Although the use of a low or no tax company for holding or intra-group financing purposes does not imply that they are being used for BEPS purposes, a closer analysis of the data related to these structures may well provide useful insights on the use of certain regimes to channel investments and intra-group financing from one country to another through conduit structures. This includes, for example, issues related to reduction of source and residence country taxation of dividends and interest during the course of the investment and the taxation of capital gains upon exit.

A review of recent studies relating to BEPS

There are a number of recent studies that have analysed MNEs' effective tax rates (ETRs) in an attempt to demonstrate the existence of BEPS behaviour or the absence of such behaviour. In most cases, these studies use backward-looking approaches and firm-level data. Some studies, mostly from the United States, used data from taxpayers' returns. Other studies focused on other data, such as investment flows and positions, to investigate the extent of BEPS. Annex B contains summaries of the conclusions of these studies.

The difference between statutory corporate income tax rates and ETR is often a source of misunderstanding in the public debate. Box 2.1 clarifies the difference between these two concepts and outlines different approaches to calculate effective tax rates.

Box 2.1. Statutory corporate income tax rates versus effective corporate income tax rates

A country's statutory corporate income tax rate is the rate specified in a country's tax law that is applied to a corporation's taxable income in order to determine the amount of the taxpayer's tax liability. It is often referred to as the "headline rate", and cannot be taken alone as a reliable indicator of the effective tax burden on income generated at the corporate level. Indeed, the corporate tax actually due depends on various tax base rules applicable in determining the corporate taxable income, which may be narrowly or broadly defined. Generous tax allowances deducted against the base, for example, may yield an effective corporate tax rate that is well below what the statutory rate suggests. Timing issues are also relevant, where for example depreciation of capital costs for tax purposes is accelerated relative to book/accounting or economic depreciation. Tax planning strategies used by companies to minimise corporate tax may also significantly reduce the corporate tax base and thus the tax actually due.

The (backward-looking) ETR of a company is generally understood as the ratio of corporate income tax to a pre-tax measure of corporate profit over a given period of time. Backward-looking indicators are attractive, in principle, being based on measures of actual taxes paid, and therefore capturing the range of factors impacting actual tax liability (statutory provisions, as well as tax-planning), although it may be difficult to establish how far the effective rate is below the statutory rate by design (*e.g.* accelerated depreciation) or because of tax planning. On the other hand, an effective rate calculated on this basis may not reflect tax planning strategies that also depress the pre-tax profit in the country of measurement. Comparisons within industries and other approaches may assist in highlighting whether these factors are an issue. Forward-looking effective corporate tax rates are derived from modeling a hypothetical investment project on a discounted cash flow basis and taking account of all the relevant tax provisions. Marginal effective corporate tax rates examine the tax treatment of pre-tax returns on the last unit of capital invested (where economic profit is exhausted) and in effect estimate how tax affects a firm's cost of capital (*i.e.* the minimum required rate of return on an investment project). Average effective corporate tax rates are most helpful where businesses (particularly MNEs) have a choice about the country in which they could locate discrete, infra-marginal projects that yield more than the cost of capital. Forward-looking indicators can capture all the main statutory provisions impacting tax

Box 2.1. **Statutory corporate income tax rates versus effective corporate income tax rates** *(continued)*

liability, and recent OECD work has developed approaches to factor in effects of cross-border tax planning (including the shifting of profits on cross-border investment).*

* Over the past two decades, the CTPA has released two publications reporting forward-looking effective tax rates on investment. A landmark publication, *Taxing Profits in a Global Economy* (OECD, 1991) reports forward-looking effective tax rates on cross-border direct investment between OECD countries, based on standard King-Fullerton methodology (1984). More recently, the CTPA released a second publication, *Tax Effects on Foreign Direct Investment – Recent Evidence and Policy Analysis* (OECD, 2007) which develops an approach for incorporating cross-border tax planning strategies into a forward-looking effective tax rate model. The analysis reports illustrative average effective tax rates on cross-border investment using intermediaries located in no/ low-tax countries that are well below effective tax rates measured under the conventional approach, used, for example, in *Taxing Profits in a Global Economy*. Other chapters of the publication provide an overview of various models used to analyse tax effects on FDI, review empirical studies attempting to measure the sensitivity of FDI to taxation, and report main policy considerations in the taxation of inbound and outbound investment. Work on forward-looking effective tax rates on investment has also been carried out by the EU. For example, *Effective Tax Rates in an Enlarged European Union* (EU, 2008) extends the scope of the calculation of ETRs conducted under the *Company Tax Study* (EU, 2001). It examines the effects of tax reforms in the EU for the period 1998-2007 and their impact on the level of taxation for both domestic and cross-border investment.

Source: OECD.

A number of observations emerge from a review of these studies, namely that:

- **There are a number of studies and data indicating that there is increased segregation between the location where actual business activities and investment take place and the location where profits are reported for tax purposes.** Actual business activities are generally identified through elements such as sales, workforce, payroll, and fixed assets. Studies that have analysed aggregated data on global investment positions between countries show that this segregation is indeed taking place, with in particular profits from mobile activities being increasingly shifted to where they benefit from a favourable tax treatment. However, because the underlying accounting data may not reflect some of the most important assets, namely mobile assets, these studies cannot be regarded as providing more than circumstantial evidence of the existence of BEPS.

- **Consistently measured ETRs could in principle provide useful indications of whether BEPS is indeed taking place.** However, data-based measures of ETRs conflate a number of factors and the existing studies have not been able to give an indication of whether an extremely low ETR is the result of aggressive tax planning strategies put in place by the taxpayer or the very achievement of the government policy that a given incentive was meant to promote (*e.g.* in the case of accelerated depreciation for certain fixed assets).[7] Where the government is supporting a particular activity through special tax provisions, the taxes paid will naturally be reduced and thus the ETR, expressed as a function of pre-tax financial accounting income, which does not reflect those provisions, will necessarily be lower.
- **Available studies on the ETRs of MNEs are useful, but there are hardly two studies using the same methodology.** Key differences relate to which taxes are taken into account in the calculation (*e.g.* cash taxes or accrued taxes), which measure of profits is used, which companies are selected, and the time period covered. In addition, for backward-looking ETRs, the steps required to achieve compatibility of numerator (tax) and denominator (pre-tax profit) amounts are limited by the availability of data. In fact, in some cases the analysis seems to have actually been driven by the available data rather than by an objectively reliable methodology, and the available data may simply not be sufficient to indicate the level of BEPS that actually exists.
- **The use of different methodologies to calculate ETRs (in particular backward-looking ones) and shortcomings in the available data result in very divergent conclusions regarding the level of taxation imposed on MNEs and the prevalence of BEPS behaviours.** Studies in relation to the same country or region arrive at very different, and in some cases opposite, results. In some instances, the methodology chosen and the data used seem to be driven more by the intention to support a given conclusion than to achieve a conclusion on the basis of the analysis.

Notes

1. See OECD (2012), *Revenue Statistics 1965-2011.*

2. In this respect, see for example European Commission (2007), "The corporate income tax rate-revenue paradox: Evidence in the EU", Taxation papers,

Working paper No. 12 – 2007 and Sorensen, P.B. (2006), "Can capital income taxes survive? And should they?", CESifo Economic Studies, 53.2: 172-228.

3. a. Footnote by Turkey

The information in this document with reference to "Cyprus" relates to the southern part of the Island. There is no single authority representing both Turkish and Greek Cypriot people on the Island. Turkey recognizes the Turkish Republic of Northern Cyprus (TRNC). Until a lasting and equitable solution is found within the context of United Nations, Turkey shall preserve its position concerning the "Cyprus issue".

b. Footnote by all the European Union Member States of the OECD and the European Union

The Republic of Cyprus is recognized by all members of the United Nations with the exception of Turkey. The information in this document relates to the area under the effective control of the Government of the Republic of Cyprus.

4. FDI positions (stock) are composed of equity and debt (intercompany loans) and represent the value of the stock of direct investments held at the end of the reference period (year, quarter, or month).

5. The country selection appears to be based on which countries are in a position to break these data down.

6. The OECD definition of SPEs is as follows: "Multinational enterprises (MNEs) often diversify their investments geographically through various organisational structures. These may include certain types of Special Purpose Entities. Examples are financing subsidiaries, conduits, holding companies, shell companies, shelf companies and brass-plate companies. Although there is no universal definition of SPEs, they do share a number of features. They are all legal entities that have little or no employment, or operations, or physical presence in the jurisdiction in which they are created by their parent enterprises which are typically located in other jurisdictions (economies). They are often used as devices to raise capital or to hold assets and liabilities and usually do not undertake significant production. An enterprise is usually considered as an SPE if it meets the following criteria: *(i)* The enterprise is a legal entity, a. Formally registered with a national authority; and b. subject to fiscal and other legal obligations of the economy in which it is resident. *(ii)* The enterprise is ultimately controlled by a non-resident parent, directly or indirectly. *(iii)* The enterprise has no or few employees, little or no production in the host economy and little or no physical presence. *(iv)* Almost all the assets and liabilities of the enterprise represent investments in or from other countries. *(v)* The core business of the enterprise consists of group financing or holding activities, that is – viewed from the perspective of the compiler in a given country – the channelling of funds from non-residents to other non-residents. However, in its daily activities, managing and directing plays only a minor role." See the 4th Edition of the OECD Benchmark Definition of Foreign Direct Investment.

7. Forward-looking average effective corporate tax rates are in this respect more attractive in that they are transparent, being derived from formulae that are a function of tax parameters embedded in the model. However, as the tax derivations and resulting effective tax rate measures are notional, reflecting assumptions of the application of tax laws and financing, tax-planning and repatriation structures that may be given inappropriate weight in the model, there is generally considerable uncertainty over how representative the measures are. Further, they do not provide a picture of taxpayers' behaviour and therefore are of limited use to ascertain whether taxpayers do engage in aggressive strategies aimed at BEPS.

Chapter 3

Global business models, competitiveness, corporate governance and taxation

This chapter describes developments in the economy that have had an impact on the way businesses are organised and, as a consequence, on the management of their tax affairs. It also discusses the often relevant issue of country competitiveness and the impact these developments have on the rules for the taxation of cross-border activities.

Global business models and taxation

Globalisation is not new, but the pace of integration of national economies and markets has increased substantially in recent years. The free movement of capital and labour, the shift of manufacturing bases from high-cost to low-cost locations, the gradual removal of trade barriers, technological and telecommunication developments, and the ever-increasing importance of managing risks and of developing, protecting and exploiting intellectual property, have had an important impact on the way MNEs are structured and managed. This has resulted in a shift from country-specific operating models to global models based on matrix management organisations and integrated supply chains that centralise several functions at a regional or global level. Moreover, the growing importance of the service component of the economy, and of digital products that often can be delivered over the Internet, has made it possible for businesses to locate many productive activities in geographic locations that are distant from the physical location of their customers.

In today's MNEs the individual group companies undertake their activities within a framework of group policies and strategies that are set by the group as a whole. The separate legal entities forming the group operate as a single integrated enterprise following an overall business strategy. Management personnel may be geographically dispersed rather than being located in a single central location, with reporting lines and decision-making processes going beyond the legal structure of the MNE.

Global value chains (GVCs), characterised by the fragmentation of production across borders, have become a dominant feature of today's global economy, encompassing emerging as well as developed economies. Figure 3.1 is a simple illustration of these chains. Increasingly, the pattern of trade shows that a good produced in Economy 1 and exported to its market of final consumption involves inputs supplied by producers in other economies who themselves source their inputs from third economies.

Figure 3.1. **A simplified representation of a global value chain**

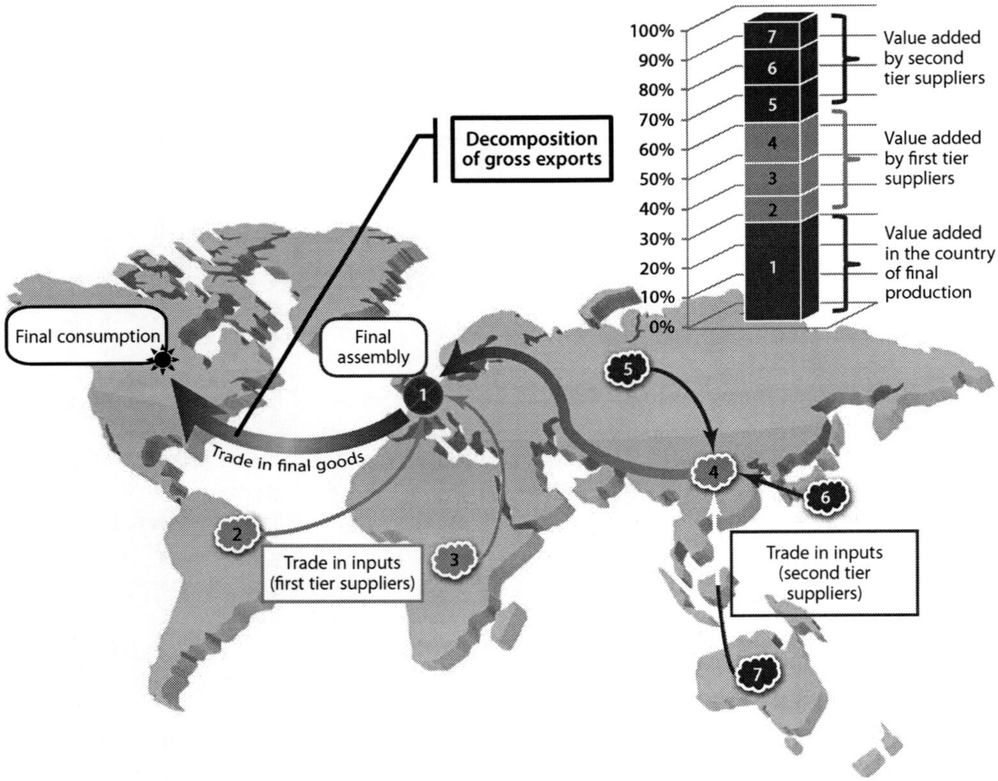

Source: OECD (2012), "Global Value Chains: OECD Work on Measuring Trade in Value-Added and Beyond", internal working document, Statistics Directorate, OECD, Paris.

Another simple way to illustrate this is to consider how many production stages are involved to produce a given good or service. Figure 3.2 gives an average of these indices for all economies. Using an index that takes the value of 1 when there is a single stage of production in a single economy, the figure illustrates that supply chains in some sectors are long and that a significant share of this unbundling of production is international. The fragmentation of production is especially important in manufacturing industries but services are also increasingly produced within GVCs.

Figure 3.2. **Index of the relative length of Global Value Chains, world average, selected industries, 2008**

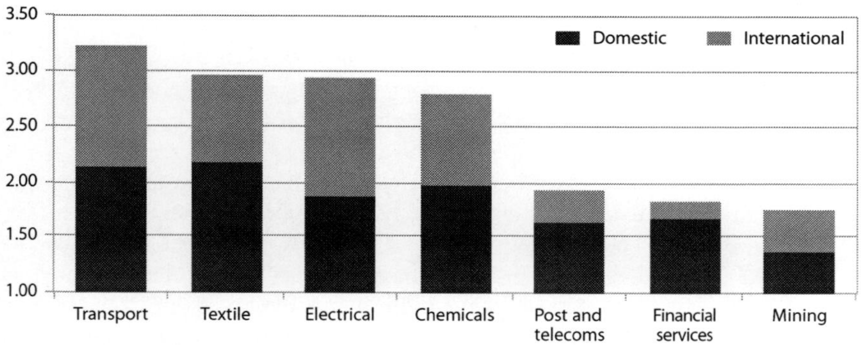

Source: OECD (2012), "Global Value Chains: OECD Work on Measuring Trade in Value-Added and Beyond", internal working document, Statistics Directorate, OECD, Paris.

The rise of GVCs has also changed the notion of what economies do and what they produce. It is increasingly less relevant to talk about the gross goods or services that are exported, while it is increasingly relevant to talk about tasks and stages of production. In a world where stages and tasks matter more than the final products being produced, GVCs also challenge orthodox notions of where economies find themselves on the value-added curve. From an economic point of view, most of the value of a good or service is typically created in upstream activities where product design, R&D or production of core components occur, or in the tail-end of downstream activities where marketing or branding occurs. Knowledge-based assets, such as intellectual property, software and organisational skills, have become increasingly important for competitiveness and for economic growth and employment.

Globalisation has in effect caused products and operational models to evolve, creating the conditions for the development of global strategies aimed at maximising profits and minimising expenses and costs, including tax expenses. At the same time, the rules on the taxation of profits from cross-border activities have remained fairly unchanged, with the principles developed in the past still finding application in domestic and international tax rules (see also the second section of Chapter 4). In other words, the changes in business practices brought about by globalisation and digitalisation of the economy have raised questions among governments about whether the domestic and international rules on the taxation of cross-border profits have kept pace with those changes. Beyond cases of illegal abuses, which are the exception rather than the rule, MNEs engaged in BEPS comply with the legal requirements of the countries involved. Governments recognise this and also recognise that a change in this legal framework can only be achieved through international co-operation.

Competitiveness and taxation

Liberalisation of trade, the abolition of currency controls and technological advances have all contributed to a dramatic increase in the flows of capital and investments among countries. This has created unprecedented interconnectedness at all levels: individuals, businesses and governments. In striving to improve their competitive positions, businesses bring about the changes in investment, technological improvements and higher productivity that enable improvements in living standards. For a corporation, being competitive means to be able to sell the best products at the best price, so as to increase its profits and shareholder value. In this respect, it is just natural that investments will be made where profitability is the highest and that tax is one of the factors of profitability, and as such tax affects decisions on where and how to invest.

From a government perspective, globalisation means that domestic policies, including tax policy, cannot be designed in isolation, *i.e.* without taking into account the effects on other countries' policies and the effects of other countries' policies on its own ones. In today's world, the interaction of countries' domestic policies becomes fundamental. Tax policy is not only the expression of national sovereignty but it is at the core of this sovereignty, and each county is free to devise its tax system in the way it considers most appropriate. Tax policy and administration influence many of the drivers of increased productivity, ranging from investment in skills, capital equipment and technical know-how to the amount of resources required to administer and comply with the tax regime.

Governments work to ensure the highest level of growth for the highest level of well being. Growth depends on investments, which includes foreign investments. As investments take into account, together with several other factors, taxation, governments are often under pressure to offer a competitive tax environment. As already indicated in earlier OECD studies,[1] experience shows that so-called "international competitiveness" concerns and pressures are felt in virtually all countries to somehow accommodate a relatively low corporate tax burden. Concerns over international competitiveness are often based on claims that accommodating treatment is available elsewhere.

Governments have long accepted that there are limits and that they should not engage in harmful tax practices. In 1998, the OECD issued a report on harmful tax practices in part based on the recognition that a "race to the bottom" would ultimately drive applicable tax rates on certain mobile sources of income to zero for all countries, whether or not this was the tax policy a country wished to pursue. It was felt that collectively agreeing on a set of common rules may in fact help countries to make their sovereign tax policy choices. The process for determining whether a regime is harmful contains three broad stages: *(i)* consideration of whether a regime is preferential and of preliminary factors, to determine whether the regime needs to be assessed; *(ii)* consideration of key factors and other factors to determine whether a preferential regime is potentially harmful; and *(iii)* consideration of the economic effects of a regime to determine whether a potentially harmful regime is actually harmful.

If a regime is considered preferential and within the scope of the work, four key factors and eight other factors are used to determine whether a preferential regime is potentially harmful. The four key factors are: *(i)* no or low effective tax rate; *(ii)* ring-fencing of the regime; *(iii)* lack of transparency; and *(iv)* lack of effective exchange of information. The eight other factors are: *(i)* an artificial definition of the tax base; *(ii)* failure to adhere to international transfer pricing principles; *(iii)* foreign source income exempt from residence country taxation; *(iv)* negotiable tax rate or tax base; *(v)* existence of secrecy provisions; *(vi)* access to a wide network of tax treaties; *(vii)* the regime is promoted as a tax minimisation vehicle; (viii) the regime encourages purely tax-driven operations or arrangements.

In order for a regime to be considered potentially harmful the first key factor, "no or low effective tax rate", must apply. This is a gateway criterion. However, an evaluation of whether a regime is potentially harmful should be based on an overall assessment of each of the factors and on its economic effects. Where a preferential regime has been found harmful, the relevant country will be given the opportunity to abolish the regime or remove the features that create the harmful effect. Where this is not done, other countries may then decide to implement defensive measures to counter the effects of the harmful regime, while at the same time continuing to encourage the country applying the regime to modify or remove it.

It is worth mentioning here that the recent past has witnessed major progress in relation to one of the four key factors, namely tax transparency.[2] The Global Forum, which since 2000 has been the multilateral framework within which work in the area transparency and exchange of information has been carried out, was fundamentally restructured in 2009 to respond to a G20 call for action in this area. Since then more than 800 agreements that provide for the exchange of information in tax matters in accordance with the internationally agreed standard have been signed, 110 peer reviews have been launched and 88 peer review reports have been completed and published. The peer review outputs include determinations regarding the availability of any relevant information in tax matters (ownership, accounting or bank information), the appropriate power of the administration to access the information and the administration's capacity to deliver this information to any partner which requests it. Moreover, since the 2012 update of article 26 of the OECD Model Tax Convention, the standard on exchange of information clearly includes group requests. Finally, in the context of Foreign Account Tax Compliance Act (FATCA) agreements, a growing number of countries are moving towards automatic exchange of information. Needless to say, these developments provide opportunities to obtain better and more accurate information on BEPS instances that in the past were often not available.

Corporate governance and taxation

A key determinant of shareholder value under current corporate reporting standards is earnings per share (EPS). An important element of EPS is tax, which means that the net effect of having an ETR of 30% is that any earnings are reduced by 30%. In other words, the ETR significantly impacts EPS and therefore has a direct impact on shareholder value. Although excluded from earnings before interest, tax depreciation and amortisation (EBITDA), the ETR also has an impact on other financial indicators used by corporate analysts, such as the return on equity (ROE) or the weighted average cost of capital (WACC), and therefore on stock valuation.

The comparison between an MNE's ETR and that of its direct competitors often generates questions and therefore increased pressure on the MNE's tax department. At the same time, increased attention is being paid to risk, including tax risk, for financial reporting purposes. For example, under United States General Accounting Principles (GAAP), tighter accounting for uncertain tax positions under FIN 48 means that provisions for uncertain tax positions have to be made if it is more likely than not that the tax administration would not accept the position taken, assuming that it was in possession of all the facts.

An exposure draft on income tax was published by the International Accounting Standards Board (IASB) in March 2009 (ED/2009/2). It proposes that "an entity shall disclose information about the major sources of estimation uncertainties relating to tax..., including: a description of the uncertainty...". To the extent that financial accounting rules may increasingly require similar forms of disclosure, this means that adopting an aggressive tax position is unlikely to have a positive impact on the ETR and the profits available for distribution that can be reported in the published accounts of the corporation in the near term. As a result, the aggressive tax position does not enhance shareholder value immediately and does increase risk, including the reputational risk, if the tax planning becomes public, for example because the issue is the subject of litigation.

Several countries have recently taken a number of steps to address aggressive tax planning and rules requiring such schemes to be disclosed to the administration have been adopted by a number of them. As a result, aggressive tax strategies can be detrimental to shareholders' interests, particularly in the medium-to-long term, because they are high risk and the costs of failure can be significant, also from the point of view of reputation. Furthermore, for some years now there has been a clear trend in the relationship between tax administrations and large businesses away from a purely adversarial model towards a more collaborative approach. At the basis of these co-operative compliance programmes there is an exchange of transparency for certainty, for both parties. Increased stringency of the accounting rules governing provisions for uncertain tax positions has only served to underline the commercial value of certainty.

As also recognised in the OECD Guidelines for Multinational Enterprises (OECD, 2011), which contain recommendations for responsible business conduct that the 44 adhering governments encourage their enterprises to observe wherever they operate, enterprises should treat tax governance and tax compliance as important elements of their oversight and broader risk management systems. In particular, corporate boards should adopt tax risk management strategies to ensure that the financial, regulatory and reputational risks associated with taxation are fully identified and evaluated. The guidelines underline that it is important that enterprises contribute to the public finances of host countries by making timely payment of their tax liabilities and recommend that enterprises comply with both the letter and spirit of the tax laws and regulations of the countries in which they operate.[3]

Notes

1. See OECD Tax Policy Studies No. 17, Tax Effects on Foreign Direct Investment, Recent Evidence and Policy Analysis, OECD (2007), p. 12

2. Note that in 2001 the Committee on Fiscal Affairs decided that commitments would be sought only in relation to the transparency and effective exchange of information criteria to determine which jurisdictions are considered as uncooperative tax havens. See *The OECD's Project on Harmful Tax Practices: The 2001 Progress Report* (OECD, 2011).

3. OECD (2011), *OECD Guidelines for Multinational Enterprises,* OECD Publishing, Paris.

Chapter 4

Key tax principles and opportunities for base erosion and profit shifting

This section contains an overview of some of the key principles that underlie the taxation of profits from cross-border activities and the BEPS opportunities these principles may create. It then shows how this theoretical framework translates in practice through the analysis of some well-known corporate tax structures (described in more detail in Annex C). It concludes that current rules provide opportunities to associate more profits with legal constructs and intangible rights and obligations, and to legally shift risk intra-group, with the result of reducing the share of profits associated with substantive operations.

Key principles for the taxation of cross-border activities

The set of rules that affect the tax treatment of cross-border activities is constituted primarily by domestic tax law rules, and also by double tax treaties and other international law instruments, such as those applicable in the European Union (Regulations, Directives, etc.). It is possible to identify a number of principles contained in these rules that assume key relevance when examining issues related to BEPS. These key principles include jurisdiction to tax, transfer pricing, leverage and anti-avoidance.

Jurisdiction to tax

The right to tax is traditionally based on a factor that determines connection to a jurisdiction. Jurisdiction to tax is exercised on an entity by entity basis, not on a group-wide basis, subject to the exception of the availability of domestic group consolidation regimes.[1] In broad terms, tax systems are often divided into worldwide and territorial ones. A worldwide taxation system generally subjects to tax its residents on their worldwide income, *i.e.* derived from sources within and outside of its territory (including the income earned through controlled foreign subsidiaries) and non-residents on the income derived from its territory. On the other hand, a territorial system generally subjects to tax both residents and non-residents only on the income derived from sources located in its territory. In the majority of countries, neither the worldwide nor the territorial system is employed in a pure form and no two tax systems are exactly the same.

The interaction of domestic tax systems sometimes leads to an overlap, which means that an item of income can be taxed by more than one jurisdiction thus resulting in double taxation. The interaction can also leave gaps, which result in an item of income not being taxed anywhere thus resulting in so called "double non-taxation". Corporations have urged bilateral and multilateral co-operation among countries to address differences in tax rules that result in double taxation, while simultaneously exploiting difference that result in double non-taxation.

Domestic and international rules to address double taxation, many of which originated with principles developed by the League of Nations in the 1920s, aim at addressing overlaps that result in double taxation so as to minimise trade distortions and impediments to sustainable economic growth. Whilst there are significant differences between the more than 3 000 bilateral tax treaties currently in force, the principles underlying the treaty provisions governing the taxation of business profits are relatively uniform. Under the rules of tax treaties, liability to a country's tax first depends on whether or not the taxpayer that derives the relevant income is a resident of that country. Residence, for treaty purposes, depends on liability to tax under the domestic law of the taxpayer. A company is considered to be a resident of a State if it is liable to tax, in that State, by reason of factors (*e.g.* domicile, residence, incorporation or place of management) that trigger the widest domestic tax liability. Most if not all treaties provide that any resident taxpayer may be taxed on its business profits wherever arising (subject to the requirement that the residence country eliminate residence-source double taxation) whilst, as a general rule, non-resident taxpayers may only be taxed on their business profits when certain conditions are met.

Treaty rules for taxing business profits use the concept of permanent establishment as a basic nexus/threshold rule for determining whether or not a country has taxing rights with respect to the business profits of a non-resident taxpayer. However, some categories of profits may be taxed in a country even though there is no permanent establishment therein. These include: *(i)* profits derived from immovable property, which, in all or almost all treaties, may be taxed by the country of source where the immovable property is located; *(ii)* profits that include certain types of payments which, depending on the treaty, may include dividends, interest, royalties or technical fees, on which the treaty allows the country of source to levy a limited tax based on the gross amount of the payment (as opposed to the profit element related to the payment); *(iii)* under some treaties, profits derived from collecting insurance premiums or insuring risks in the source country; *(iv)* under some treaties, profits derived from the provision of services if the presence of the provider in the country of source meets certain conditions. The permanent establishment concept also acts as a source rule to the extent that, as a general rule, the only business profits of a non-resident that may be taxed by a country are those that are attributable to a permanent establishment.

Arguments in favour or against the existing treaty rules are often based on certain assumptions regarding where business profits ought to be taxed. As regards tax treaties, the consideration of that issue goes back to the work of the International Chamber of Commerce and the League of Nations in the 1920s, and in particular to a 1927 report of an international Committee of Technical Experts, which led to the adoption of the major rules which are now reflected in the OECD and UN Model Tax Convention and on which most current tax treaties are based.

A number of theoretical arguments can be used to argue that income should generally be taxed exclusively in the State of residence. This approach, among others, was reviewed and rejected by a group of economists (the "Economists") appointed by the League of Nations to study the question of double taxation from a theoretical and scientific point of view. In place of these theories, the 1923 *Economists Report* posited that taxation should be based on a doctrine of economic allegiance: "whose purpose was to weigh the various contributions made by different states to the production and enjoyment of income" (Graetz & O'Hear, 1997). In general, the Economists concluded that the most important factors (in different proportions depending on the class of income at issue) were *(i)* the origin of the wealth (*i.e.* source) and *(ii)* where the wealth was spent (*i.e.* residence). The origin or production of wealth was defined for these purposes as all the stages involved in the creation of wealth. As noted by the Economists, "these stages up to the point where wealth reaches fruition may be shared in by different territorial authorities"[2] (OECD, 2005). This "origin of wealth" principle has remained a primary basis for taxation until today.

However, developments brought about by the digital economy are putting increasing pressure on these well-established principles and in particular on the concept of permanent establishment. It had already been recognised way in the past that the concept of permanent establishment referred not only to a substantial physical presence in the country concerned, but also to situations where the non-resident carried on business in the country concerned via a dependent agent (hence the rules contained in paragraphs 5 and 6 of Article 5 of the OECD Model). Nowadays it is possible to be heavily involved in the economic life of another country, *e.g.* by doing business with customers located in that country via the internet, without having a taxable presence therein (such as substantial physical presence or a dependent agent). In an era where non-resident taxpayers can derive substantial profits from transactions with customers located in another country, questions are being raised as to whether the current rules ensure a fair allocation of taxing rights on business profits, especially where the profits from such transactions go untaxed anywhere.

Transfer pricing

The issue of jurisdiction to tax is closely linked with the one of measurement of profits: once it has been established that a share of an enterprise's profits can be considered to originate from a country and that the country should be allowed to tax it, it is necessary to have rules for the determination of the relevant share of the profits which will be subjected to taxation. Transfer pricing rules perform this function. The internationally accepted principle underlying transfer pricing determinations is the arm's length principle, which requires that for tax purposes, related parties must allocate income as it would be allocated between independent entities in the same or similar circumstances.

When independent enterprises transact with each other, the conditions of the transaction are generally determined by market forces. When associated enterprises transact with each other, their relations may not be directly affected by market forces in the same way. The objective of the arm's length principle is for the price and other conditions of transactions between associated enterprises to be consistent with those that would occur between unrelated enterprises for comparable transactions under comparable circumstances. In transactions between two independent enterprises, compensation usually will reflect the functions that each enterprise performs, taking into account assets used and risks assumed. Therefore, in determining whether controlled and uncontrolled transactions or entities are comparable, a comparability analysis is needed to ensure that the economically relevant characteristics of the situations being compared are sufficiently comparable. One of the key factors in that comparability analysis is a functional analysis to identify and compare the economically significant activities and responsibilities undertaken, assets used and risks assumed by the parties to the transactions.

This principle, originally developed by the League of Nations, is contained in the domestic legislation of most countries and is embodied in Article 7 and Article 9 of the OECD and UN Model Treaties and in virtually all double taxation treaties. The OECD Transfer Pricing Guidelines for Multinational Enterprises and Tax Administrations ("the Guidelines") and the OECD Report on the Attribution of Profits to Permanent Establishments provide guidance on how to apply Articles 7 and 9 of treaties based on the

OECD Model Tax Convention. The first report of the OECD on transfer pricing was issued in 1979. In 1995, the report was replaced by new extensive guidelines. The introduction of the Guidelines was followed by the recognition that it was necessary to set in place explicit transfer pricing legislation, including documentation requirements. As a consequence, more and more governments introduced transfer pricing legislation and related documentation requirements. Although the large majority of domestic transfer pricing systems are based on the arm's length principle, each domestic system has its own specificities and reflects domestic country positions on transfer pricing.

The Guidelines have been updated several times since 1995. The updates reflect the growing experience and expertise gained on transfer pricing matters.

Leverage

Most countries make a fundamental distinction between the tax treatment of debt and that of equity. Debt is generally regarded as a resource that does not belong to the company and therefore, subject to certain conditions, interest on such debt is treated as deductible for tax purposes. On the other hand, the remuneration that a company pays to its shareholders in the form of dividends is generally not tax-deductible. This unsurprisingly may lead to a tax-induced bias toward debt finance as well as to attempts to characterise particular payments as deductible interest in the payer's jurisdiction and as dividends (that may not be taxed) in the jurisdiction of the recipient.

Anti-avoidance

Measures that negate or reduce the tax benefit sought, as well as initiatives aimed at influencing taxpayer's and third parties' behaviours, are of obvious relevance in the area of corporate tax planning. In practice, there are a variety of anti-avoidance strategies that countries use to ensure the fairness and effectiveness of their corporate tax system. These strategies often focus on deterring, detecting and responding to aggressive tax planning. Deterrence strategies generally aim at discouraging taxpayers from taking an aggressive position. Such deterrence strategies include, for example, influencing taxpayers through the issuance of public rulings, applying promoter penalties, imposing additional reporting obligations, as well as implementing effective mass communication strategies. Detection strategies aim to ensure the availability of timely, targeted and comprehensive information, which traditional audits alone can no longer deliver. The availability of such information is important to allow governments to identify risk areas in a timely manner and be able to quickly decide whether and how to respond, thus providing increased certainty to taxpayers.

In terms of response strategies, the ultimate objective of anti-avoidance measures is often not only to counter behaviour perceived as inappropriate but also to influence future behaviour. In other words, anti-avoidance measures are fundamental policy prohibitions to engage in certain planning and/or to obtain certain results. The most relevant anti-avoidance rules in domestic tax systems include:

- **General anti-avoidance rules or doctrines**, which limit or deny the availability of undue tax benefits, for example, in situations where transactions lack economic substance or a non-tax business purpose;
- **Controlled foreign company rules**, under which certain base eroding or "tainted" income derived by a non-resident controlled entity is attributed to and taxed currently to the domestic shareholders regardless of whether the income has been repatriated to them;
- **Thin capitalisation and other rules limiting interest deductions**, which disallow the deduction of certain interest expenses when, *e.g.* the debt-to-equity ratio of the debtor is considered to be excessive;
- **Anti-hybrid rules**, which link the domestic tax treatment with the tax treatment in that foreign country thus eliminating the possibility for mismatches;
- **Anti-base erosion rules**, which impose higher withholding taxes on, or deny the deductibility of, certain payments (*e.g.* those made to entities located in certain jurisdictions).

Anti-avoidance rules are also often found in bilateral tax treaties, so as to reduce the risk of abuse of treaties by persons who were not intended to benefit from them, *e.g.* through the use of conduit companies. Some countries expressly include in their treaty provisions that aim at counteracting this type of abuse. Typical provisions include those specifically aimed at denying the benefits of the treaty to certain entities, provisions which are aimed at particular types of income, provisions which are aimed at preferential regimes introduced after the signature of the treaty and provisions designed to protect the tax base of countries concluding treaties with low-tax jurisdictions. For EU members, additional issues arise as witnessed by the numerous decisions of the European Court of Justice on tax matters and the recent work done by the EC Commission in the area of double non-taxation.[3]

Key principles and BEPS opportunities

While the specific goals will vary among MNEs, in particular with respect to companies headquartered in different jurisdictions, broadly speaking BEPS focuses on moving profits to where they are taxed at lower rates and expenses to where they are relieved at higher rates. Specific strategies may also be put in place to make use of existing "tax attributes" such as tax credits, loss-carry forwards, etc.[4] These generic goals are often achieved in a way that aligns with the overall management of the treasury operations of the group, *e.g.* in terms of cash management, management of foreign exchange risks and efficient repatriation strategies. The following paragraphs describe some typical BEPS opportunities created by the existence and interaction of rules based on the key principles described above.

Jurisdiction to tax

Every jurisdiction is free to set up its corporate tax system as it chooses. States have the sovereignty to implement tax measures that raise revenues to pay for the expenditures they deem necessary. An important challenge relates to the need to ensure that tax does not produce unintended and distortive effects on cross-border trade and investment nor that it distorts competition and investment within each country by disadvantaging domestic players. In a globalised world where economies are increasingly integrated, domestic tax systems designed in isolation are often not aligned with each other, thus creating room for mismatches. As already mentioned, these mismatches may result in double taxation and may also result in double non-taxation. In other words, these mismatches may in effect make income disappear for tax purposes. This leads to a reduction of the overall tax paid by all parties involved as a whole. Although it is often difficult to determine which of the countries involved has lost tax revenue, it is clear that collectively the countries concerned lose tax revenue. Further, this undermines competition, as some businesses, such as those which operate cross-border and have access to sophisticated tax expertise, may profit from these opportunities and have unintended competitive advantages compared with other businesses, such as small and medium-sized enterprises, that operate mostly at the domestic level.

Considering how tax systems interact with each other is therefore relevant not only to eliminate obstacles to cross-border trade and investment, but also to limit the scope for unintended non-taxation. Further, double tax treaties, which are bilateral tools that countries use to co-ordinate the exercise of their respective taxing rights, may also create opportunities for taxpayers to obtain tax advantages in the form of lower or no taxation at source and/or lower or no taxation in the state of residence of the taxpayer.

Although the most immediate way to achieve low or no taxation at the level of the recipient is to shift income to an entity in a low-tax jurisdiction, the same results may be achieved in a number of other ways, also between high-tax countries. These alternatives, although more complex, often entail additional tax benefits, *e.g.* in terms of claiming a full deduction at the level of the payer, the potential reduction or elimination of (withholding) taxes at source, and the non-applicability of anti-avoidance rules in the source or residence country (*e.g.* because these rules may only target strategies using low-tax jurisdictions).

The paragraphs below describe ways in which the current rules can be applied to achieve low or no-taxation, mostly in relation to financing:

- **Low-taxed branch of a foreign company:** a company can be set up in what is ostensibly a high tax jurisdiction, but can achieve a low effective tax rate on the income received by providing loans (licences or services) through a foreign branch that is subject to a low-tax regime. In general, this requires that the country in which the "head office" is set up operates an exemption system for foreign branches, either under domestic law or under double tax treaties. The low-tax in the branch can be achieved in different ways: *(i)* the country of the branch levies a low or zero tax rate on the income; *(ii)* unlike the country of the head office, the country of the branch regards the activities carried on therein as not being sufficiently significant to create a taxable presence of the foreign company; *(iii)* unlike the country of the head office, the country of the branch gives a deduction for deemed interest on the branch's capital.
- **Hybrid entities:** low taxation at the level of a finance (or IP) company that operates purely in high-tax countries can be achieved through the use of hybrid entities. A hybrid entity is an entity that is treated as a taxable person in one country but as "transparent" in another country (*i.e.* in the other country the profits or losses of the entity are taxed/deducted at the level of the members). For example, assume that an entity organised in Country B receives a loan from its parent company in Country A. The entity in Country B is treated as non-transparent in Country B while it is treated as transparent in Country A. This mismatch in treatment allows the group to claim a deduction in Country B for a payment that is not taxed in Country A (because that country sees no income at the level of the recipient). It should be kept in mind that double taxation could occur in this situation if the treatment of the entity had been inversed in the two countries.
- **Hybrid financial instruments and other financial transactions:** Similar results can be achieved through the use of hybrid instruments. These are financial instruments that present features typically connected

with debt but also features typically connected with equity. Assume that a company in Country A buys financial instruments issued by a company in Country B. Under Country A's tax laws, the instrument is treated as equity, whereas for Country B's tax purposes the instrument is regarded as a debt instrument. Payments under the instrument are considered to be deductible interest expenses for the company under Country B tax law while the corresponding receipts are treated as dividends for Country A tax purposes and therefore exempt therein. Other financial transactions including those involving captive insurance or derivatives can give rise to similar outcomes of payments being deductible in one country, but not being taxed in another country.

Further, country taxation at source can often be reduced or eliminated through the interposition of intermediate entities in treaty jurisdictions so as to claim the benefits of the relevant tax treaty or when certain items of income, such as derivative payments, are not taxed at source:

- **Conduit companies:** the fact that the owner of the income-producing asset (*e.g.* funds or IP) is located in a low-tax jurisdiction means that in most cases where income is derived from other countries the taxing rights of the source State will not be limited by any double tax treaty. The interposition of a conduit company located in a State that has a treaty with the source State may allow the taxpayer to claim the benefits of the treaty, thus reducing or eliminating tax at source. Further, if the State of the conduit company applies no withholding tax on certain outbound payments under its domestic law or has itself a treaty with the State of the owner of the income-producing asset that provides for the elimination of withholding tax at source, the income can be repatriated to the owner of the income-producing asset without any tax at source. Taxation of the income from the funds or IP in the State of the conduit company does not take place, since the income will be offset by a corresponding deduction for the payments to the owner of the income-producing asset in the low-tax jurisdiction.
- **Derivatives:** Certain derivative instruments may be used to reduce or eliminate withholding taxes on cross-border payments. For example, fees for derivative contracts, such as forwards or interest rate swaps, may economically replace interest payments and thus avoid withholding tax at source, either because the relevant domestic law does not subject these payments to tax at source or because the relevant double tax treaty may prevent the country from taxing the income at source.

Transfer pricing

One of the underlying assumptions of the arm's length principle is that the more extensive the functions/assets/risks of one party to the transaction, the greater its expected remuneration will be and *vice versa.* This therefore creates an incentive to shift functions/assets/risks to where their returns are taxed more favorably. While it may be difficult to shift underlying functions, the risks and ownership of tangible and intangible assets may, by their very nature, be easier to shift. Many corporate tax structures focus on allocating significant risks and hard-to-value intangibles to low-tax jurisdictions, where their returns may benefit from a favorable tax regime. Such arrangements may result in or contribute to BEPS.

Shifting income through transfer pricing arrangements related to the contractual allocation of risks and intangibles often involves thorny questions. One basic question involves the circumstances under which a taxpayer's particular allocation of risk should be accepted. Transfer pricing under the arm's length standard generally respects the risk allocations adopted by related parties. Such risk allocation and the income allocation consequences asserted to follow from them can become a source of controversy. The evaluation of risk often involves discussions regarding whether, in fact, a low-tax transferee of intangibles should be treated as having borne, on behalf of the MNE group, significant risks related to the development and use of the intangibles in commercial operations. Such arguments put stress on the ability of tax administrations to examine the substance of such arrangements, and determine whether the results of such arrangements, viewed in their totality, are consistent with policy norms (*i.e.* avoidance of inappropriate base erosion). Transfer pricing rules regarding the attribution of risks and assets within a group are applied on an entity-by-entity basis, thus facilitating planning based on the isolation of risks at the level of particular members of the group. There are a number of examples of risk allocations that can be undertaken under the arm's length principle between members of an affiliated group (*e.g.* low-risk manufacturing and distribution, contract R&D and captive insurance)

Under each of these models, the principal/insurer could be located in a low-tax jurisdiction, and the service provider/insured located in a high-tax jurisdiction. A key challenge is determining the circumstances under which such arrangements result in or contribute to base erosion, and the principles under which the base erosion is addressed.

Arrangements relating to risk shifting raise a number of difficult transfer pricing issues. At a fundamental level they raise the question of how risk is actually distributed among the members of a MNE group and whether transfer pricing rules should easily accept contractual allocations of risk. They also raise issues related to the level of economic substance required to respect contractual allocations of risk, including questions regarding the managerial capacity to control risks and the financial capacity to bear risks. Finally, the question arises as to whether any indemnification payment should be made when risk is shifted between group members.[5]

In summary, the Guidelines are perceived by some as putting too much emphasis on legal structures (as reflected, for example, in contractual risk allocations) rather than on the underlying reality of the economically integrated group, which may contribute to BEPS.

Leverage

Current rules encourage corporations to finance themselves with debt rather equity. In fact, the differential treatment of debt versus equity both within and across countries creates an incentive for debt-financing. When a parent company and its subsidiary are subject to different tax rules, *e.g.* because they are based in different jurisdictions, the amount of equity that the parent provides to the subsidiary will affect the total tax burden borne by the group.

This creates an obvious bias towards debt financing, particularly when this is combined with low-taxation at the level of the recipient. A typical case involves setting up a finance operation in a low-tax country (or in a way that synthetically achieves the same result, see above in relation to hybrid mismatches) to fund the activities of the other group companies. The result is that the payments are deducted against the taxable profits of the high-taxed operating companies while taxed favourably or not being taxed at all at the level of the recipient thus allowing for a reduction of the total tax burden. Leveraging high-tax group companies with intra-group debt is a very simple and straightforward way to achieve tax savings at group level.

Anti-avoidance

Rules obviously differ from country to country and many of the differences can be explained by different legal traditions, level of sophistication of the tax system and national courts' approaches to the interpretation of tax law. Considering the difficulties in precisely identifying the dividing line between what it is aggressive and what is not, domestic and treaty-based anti-avoidance provisions constitute the benchmark against which to decide whether a given strategy should be implemented (from the perspective of the taxpayer) or should be challenged (from the perspective of the revenue authorities). Further, situations which cannot be tackled under the existing rules, but that still generate concerns at the level of the revenue body, should be brought to the attention of tax policy officials in order to determine whether changes to the current rules need to be introduced.

In addition, there are in practice a variety of strategies which are used to escape the application of anti-avoidance rules and therefore secure an overall low-tax burden. These strategies obviously vary depending on the rule itself and also evolve over time. For example, rules such as thin capitalisation rules may be circumvented by channelling the financing through an independent third party, particularly when the relevant rules only apply to related parties. However, injecting additional equity has a cost which may seriously undermine the attractiveness of the transaction. Thin capitalisation rules may also be circumvented through the use of derivatives.

Similarly, countries have encountered several strategies to avoid the application of CFC rules. These include inversions, *i.e.* transactions through which the corporate structure of a MNE is altered so that a non-resident company typically located in a (low or no-tax) jurisdiction with no CFC regime, replaces the existing parent company at the top of the group. Along the same lines, the use of hybrid entities may make income "disappear" for tax purposes in the country of the ultimate parent, thus avoiding the application of the relevant CFC rules.

Analysis of corporate tax structures

A critical observation in any analysis of corporate tax structures is that it is often the interaction of various principles and practices that allows BEPS to occur. The interaction of withholding tax rules in one country, the territorial taxation system in another country, and the entity characterisation rules in a third country may combine to make it possible for certain transactions to occur in a way that gives rise to no current tax and have the effect of shifting income to a jurisdiction where, for various reasons, no tax is imposed. Often it is not any particular country's tax rule that creates the opportunity for BEPS, but rather the way the rules of several countries interact.

In practice any structure aimed at BEPS will need to incorporate a number of co-ordinated strategies, which often can be broken down into four elements: *(i)* minimisation of taxation in a foreign operating or source country (which is often a medium to high tax jurisdiction) either by shifting gross profits via trading structures or reducing net profit by maximising deductions at the level of the payer, *(ii)* low or no withholding tax at source, *(iii)* low or no taxation at the level of the recipient (which can be achieved via low-tax jurisdictions, preferential regimes or hybrid mismatch arrangements) with entitlement to substantial non-routine profits often built up via intra-group arrangements, as well as *(iv)* no current taxation of the low-taxed profits (achieved via the first three steps) at the level of the ultimate parent. Further, effective cash repatriation strategies may be an issue where, for instance, dividends need to be funded and of course, "permanent" foreign reinvestment of low-taxed cash will be relevant to allow booking of a particular tax rate for EPS purposes.

Any analysis of BEPS therefore needs to be cognizant of the interconnection of these elements and of their overall drivers. The structures described in Annex C have been given wide coverage in the specialised and mainstream press. They have been selected because they encapsulate a number of the opportunities created by the principles and rules described above. A number of observations emerge from an analysis of these structures, namely that:

- **Their overall effect is a tendency to associate more profit with legal constructs and intangible rights and obligations, and to legally shift risk intra-group, with the result of reducing the share of profits associated with substantive operations**. These tendencies become more pronounced over time as the economy evolves from bricks and mortar based businesses to more mobile information technology and intangibles based businesses.
- **While these corporate tax planning strategies may be technically legal and rely on carefully planned interactions of a variety of tax rules and principles, the overall effect of this type of tax planning is to erode the corporate tax base of many countries in a manner that is not intended by domestic policy**. This reflects the fact that BEPS takes advantage of a combination of features of tax systems which have been put in place by home and host countries. This implies that it may be very difficult for any single country, acting alone, to effectively combat BEPS behaviours.

Notes

1. The application of domestic group consolidation regimes may create additional mismatches between domestic and treaty law, as double tax treaties always allocate taxing rights on corporate income on a company-by-company basis, while domestic tax laws may treat the entire domestic group as a single taxpayer for domestic tax purposes.
2. See *Report on Double Taxation*, submitted to the Financial Committee by Professors Bivens, Einaudi, Seligman and Sir Josiah Stamp, League of Nations Doc E.F.S.73 F.19 (the "1923 Economists Report")
3. See also Commission Recommendation of 6 December 2012 on aggressive tax planning, C(2012) 8806 final.

4. Tax planning strategies on tax attributes generally involve strategies aimed at securing, increasing and/or accelerating tax relief and are very dependent on specific country rules. Regarding tax planning on tax attributes, a recent OECD report describes a number of aggressive tax planning schemes on losses (OECD, 2011, *Corporate Loss Utilisation through Aggressive Tax Planning*). These schemes aim at achieving a variety of results, such as the rules on the recognition or treatment of losses, shifting losses to a profitable party or profits to a loss-making party, circumventing restrictions on the carry-over of losses, creating artificial losses and pursuing the dual/multiple use of the same loss.

5. The OECD Transfer Pricing Guidelines have touched upon these issues in the context of work on business restructuring. These issues are also being addressed in connection with ongoing work on intangibles.

Chapter 5

Addressing concerns related to base erosion and profit shifting

Although further work on data that may provide useful indications of the magnitude of the issues related to BEPS is needed, it is evident from a number of indicators that BEPS is indeed taking place, and it poses a threat in terms of tax sovereignty and of tax revenue. As also shown by the G20 statements in 2012, these issues are relevant not only for industrialised countries, but also for emerging and developing ones.

Beyond a number of high-profile cases, there is a more fundamental policy issue: the international common principles drawn from national experiences to share tax jurisdiction may not have kept pace with the changing business environment. Domestic rules for international taxation and internationally agreed standards are still grounded in an economic environment characterised by a lower degree of economic integration across borders, rather than today's environment of global taxpayers, which is characterised by the increasing importance of intellectual property as a value-driver and by constant developments of information and communication technologies. For example, some rules and their underlying policy were built on the assumption that one country would forgo taxation because another country would be imposing tax. In the modern global economy, this assumption is not always correct, as planning opportunities may result in profits ending up untaxed anywhere.

Key pressure areas

In addition to a clear need for increased transparency on effective tax rates of MNEs, **key pressure areas include** those related to:

- **International mismatches in entity and instrument characterisation** including hybrid mismatch arrangements and arbitrage;
- **Application of treaty concepts to profits derived from the delivery of digital goods and services**;

- **The tax treatment of related party debt-financing, captive insurance and other inter-group financial transactions**;
- **Transfer pricing**, in particular in relation to the shifting of risks and intangibles, the artificial splitting of ownership of assets between legal entities within a group, and transactions between such entities that would rarely take place between independents;
- **The effectiveness of anti-avoidance measures**, in particular GAARs, CFC regimes, thin capitalisation rules and rules to prevent tax treaty abuse; and
- **The availability of harmful preferential regimes.**

Next steps

There is no magic recipe to address BEPS issues, but the OECD is ideally positioned to support countries' efforts to ensure effectiveness and fairness of tax rules and, at the same time, provide a certain and predictable environment for business. Countries share a common interest in establishing a level playing field among themselves, while ensuring that domestic businesses are not disadvantaged vis-à-vis multinational corporations.

Failure to collaborate in addressing BEPS issues could result in unilateral actions that would risk undermining the consensus-based framework for establishing jurisdiction to tax and addressing double taxation which exists today. The consequences could be damaging in terms of increased possibilities for mismatches, additional disputes, increased uncertainty for business, a battle to be the first to grab taxable income through purported anti-avoidance measures, or a race to the bottom with respect to corporate income taxes. In contrast, collaboration to address BEPS concerns will enhance and support individual governments' domestic policy efforts to protect their tax base while protecting multinationals from uncertainty or double taxation. In this regard, addressing BEPS in a coherent and balanced manner should take into account the perspectives of industrialised as well as emerging and developing countries.

For years the OECD has promoted dialogue and co-operation between governments on tax matters with its work on *(i)* tax transparency, *(ii)* tax treaties, *(iii)* transfer pricing, *(iv)* aggressive tax planning, *(v)* harmful tax practices, *(vi)* tax policy analyses and statistics, *(vii)* tax administration, and (viii) tax and development. Current OECD projects which are directly relevant for BEPS (outlined in Annex D) will have to be brought together in a holistic manner.

A number of indicators show that the tax practices of some multinational companies have become more aggressive over time, raising serious compliance and fairness issues. These issues were already flagged by tax commissioners at the 2006 meeting of the Forum on Tax Administration in Seoul and different instruments have been developed to better analyse and react to aggressive tax planning schemes which result in massive revenue losses. The OECD work on aggressive tax planning, including its directory of aggressive tax planning schemes, is being used by government officials from several countries. Some countries are intensively drawing on this work to improve their audit performance. Improving tax compliance, on-shore and off-shore, remains a key priority for both securing governments revenue and levelling the playing field for businesses. It requires determined action from tax administrations, which should co-operate in exchanging intelligence and information, as well as monitoring the effectiveness of the strategies used, for example in terms of additional tax revenue assessed/collected, and in terms of enhanced compliance.

This report also shows that current international tax standards may not have kept pace with changes in global business practices, in particular in the area of intangibles and the development of the digital economy. For example, today it is possible to be heavily involved in the economic life of another country, *e.g.* by doing business with customers located in that country via the internet, without having a taxable presence in that country. In an era where non-resident taxpayers can derive substantial profits from transacting with customers located in another country, questions are being raised on whether the current rules are fit for purpose. Further, as businesses increasingly integrate across borders and tax rules often remain uncoordinated, there are a number of structures, technically legal, which take advantage of asymmetries in domestic and international tax rules.

The OECD has already produced analytical work to better understand and react to the issue of hybrid mismatch arrangements through which taxable income in effect disappears (*Hybrid Mismatch Arrangements: Policy and Compliance Issues,* 2012). Work has also been launched to address some of the new challenges. Proposals to update the OECD's transfer pricing guidelines in the area of intangibles and to simplify their application have been tabled and should be advanced quickly to provide immediate responses to some of the most critical profit shifting challenges. Simplification should also ensure that tax administrations have access to better tools for assessing tax compliance risks. This involves the development of documentation requirements able to provide tax auditors with the full picture of business operations worldwide. In the recent past, the OECD also identified a number of avenues to better assess tax compliance risks, such as those described in *Tackling Aggressive Tax Planning through Improved Transparency and Disclosure* (OECD, 2011). Finally, major progress towards transparency has been achieved over the past four years. The Global Forum on Transparency and Exchange of Information for Tax Purposes will have a continuing role in providing an essential framework for work on transparency and exchange of information for tax purposes.

More fundamentally, a holistic approach is necessary to properly address the issue of BEPS. Government actions should be comprehensive and deal with all the different aspects of the issue. These include, for example, the balance between source and residence taxation, the tax treatment of intra-group financial transactions, the implementation of anti-abuse provisions, including CFC legislations, as well as transfer pricing rules. A comprehensive approach, globally supported, should draw on an in-depth analysis of the interaction of all these pressure points. It is clear that co-ordination will be key in the implementation of any solution, though countries may not all use the same instruments to address the issue of BEPS.

What is at stake is the integrity of the corporate income tax. A lack of response would further undermine competition, as some businesses, such as those which operate cross-border and have access to sophisticated tax expertise, may profit from BEPS opportunities and therefore have unintended competitive advantages compared with enterprises that operate mostly at the domestic level. In addition to issues of fairness, this may lead to an inefficient allocation of resources by distorting investment decisions towards activities that have lower pre-tax rates of return, but higher after-tax rates of return. Finally, if other taxpayers (including ordinary individuals) think that multinational corporations can legally avoid paying income tax it will undermine voluntary compliance by all taxpayers – upon which modern tax administration depends. Because many BEPS strategies take advantage of the interface between the tax rules of different countries, it may be difficult for any single country, acting alone, to fully address the issue. Furthermore, unilateral and uncoordinated actions by governments responding in isolation could result in the risk of double – and possibly multiple – taxation for business. This would have a negative impact on investment, and thus on growth and employment globally. In this context, the major challenge is not only to identify appropriate responses, but also the mechanisms to implement them in a streamlined manner, in spite of the well-known existing legal constraints, such as the existence of more than 3 000 bilateral tax treaties. It is therefore essential that countries consider innovative approaches to implement comprehensive solutions.

Developing a global action plan to address BEPS

A comprehensive action plan

In order to address base erosion and profit shifting. which is fundamentally due to a large number of interacting factors, a comprehensive action plan should be developed quickly. The main purpose of that plan would be to provide countries with instruments, domestic and international, aiming at better aligning rights to tax with real economic activity.

While it is useful to take stock of the work which has already been done and which is underway, it is also important to revisit some of the fundamentals of the existing standards. Indeed, incremental approaches may help curb the current trends but will not respond to several of the challenges governments face.

Though governments may have to provide unilateral solutions, there is value and necessity in providing an internationally co-ordinated approach. Collaboration and co-ordination will not only facilitate and reinforce domestic actions to protect tax bases, but will also be key to provide comprehensive international solutions that may satisfactorily respond to the issue. Co-ordination in that respect will also limit the need for individual jurisdictions' unilateral tax measures. Of course, jurisdictions may also provide more stringent unilateral actions to prevent BEPS than those in the co-ordinated approach.

The OECD is committed to delivering a global and comprehensive action plan based on in-depth analysis of the identified pressure areas with a view to provide concrete solutions to realign international standards with the current global business environment. This will require some "out of the box" thinking as well as ambition and pragmatism to overcome implementation difficulties, such as the existence of current tax treaties. In the meanwhile, current work will naturally be speeded up where relevant to BEPS.

Timely developed in consultation with all stakeholders...

A comprehensive solution cannot be developed without the contribution of all stakeholders. All interested member countries will have to be involved in the development of the action plan and non-member countries, in particular G20 economies, will have to contribute as well. Consultation with the business community, as well as civil society, should be organised so that the views of practitioners and other stakeholders can be taken into account and to provide businesses with the certainty they need to make long-term investment decisions.

There is an urgent need to deal with this issue and the OECD is committed to provide an innovative and timely response to it. It is proposed that an initial comprehensive action plan be developed within the next six months so that the Committee on Fiscal Affairs can examine it at its next meeting in June 2013. Such an action plan should *(i)* identify actions needed to address BEPS, *(ii)* set deadlines to implement these actions and *(iii)* identify the resources needed and the methodology to implement these actions.

To develop such a plan, the CFA has given a mandate to the CFA Bureau, together with the chairs of the relevant working groups, to work with the OECD Secretariat, in consultation with interested countries and other stakeholders. The CFA Bureau and the chairs of the working parties will call on available expertise through a series of physical or virtual meetings and will monitor the work so that a draft action plan can be submitted to the CFA in time for it to be discussed and approved at its June 2013 meeting.

Focusing on the main pressure areas

On substance, the development of the action plan should provide a comprehensive response that takes into account the links between the different pressure areas. Moreover, better information and data on BEPS will be sought.

The different components of **the action plan will include proposals to develop**:

- **Instruments to put an end or neutralise the effects of hybrid mismatch arrangements and arbitrage.**
- **Improvements or clarifications to transfer pricing rules** to address specific areas where the current rules produce undesirable results from a policy perspective. The current work on intangibles, which is a particular area of concern, would be included in a broader reflection on transfer pricing rules;
- **Updated solutions to the issues related to jurisdiction to tax, in particular in the areas of digital goods and services.** These solutions may include a revision of treaty provisions.
- **More effective anti-avoidance measures,** as a complement to the previous items. Anti-avoidance measures can be included in domestic laws or included in international instruments. Examples of these measures include general anti-avoidance rules, controlled foreign companies rules, limitation of benefits rules and other anti-treaty abuse provisions.

- **Rules on the treatment of intra-group financial transactions,** such as those related to the deductibility of payments and the application of withholding taxes.
- **Solutions to counter harmful regimes more effectively,** taking into account also factors such as transparency and substance.

The action plan will also consider the best way to implement in a timely fashion the measures governments can agree upon. If treaty changes are required, solutions for a quick implementation of these changes should be examined and proposed as well. OECD has developed standards to eliminate double taxation and should ensure that this goal is achieved while efforts are deployed to also prevent double non-taxation. In this respect, a comprehensive approach should also consider possible improvements to eliminate double taxation, such as increased efficiency of mutual agreement procedures and arbitration provisions.

* * *

Immediate action from our tax administrations is also needed

The Forum of Tax Administration gathers the Tax Commissioners of all OECD and G20 countries. The Forum will meet in Moscow in May 2013. It is expected that the Tax Commissioners will focus on and communicate on their actions to improve tax compliance, which is a pre-requisite for a fair tax environment. They are invited in particular to draw on the work developed by the OECD in the area of aggressive tax planning, with more than 400 schemes included in the aggressive tax planning directory.

Bibliography

Bloomberg, "The Great Corporate Tax Dodge", 17 March 2011, Bloomberg series, *http://topics.bloomberg.com/the-great-corporate-tax-dodge.*

G20, "Los Cabos Summit Leader's Declaration", Los Cabos, Mexico, 19 June 2012, retrieved from *www.g20.org.*

G20, "Communiqué of Finance Ministers and Central Bank Governors" Mexico City, Mexico, 4 November 2012, retrieved from *www.g20.org.*

Guardian News, "Tax Gap", Guardian News Series, retrieved from *www.guardian.co.uk/business/series/tax-gap.*

The Times, "Secrets of the Tax Avoiders", Times Series, 18 June 2012, retrieved from *www.youtube.com/watch?v=qHB3g8kvWs0.*

The White House and the Department of Treasury, "The President's Framework for Business Tax Reform", February 2012, retrieved from *www.treasury.gov/resource-center/tax-policy/Documents/The-Presidents-Framework-for-Business-Tax-Reform-02-22-2012.pdf.*

Graetz, M J & M. O'Hear, "The 'Original Intent' of U.S. International Taxation," 46

Duke Law Journal, 1021, at 1076-1077 (1997).

New York Times, "*But Nobody Pays That*", New York Times Series, December 2011, topics.nytimes.com/top/features/timestopics/series/but_nobody_pays_that/index.html

OECD (2004), *Are the Current Treaty Rules for Taxing Business Profits Appropriate for E-Commerce?,* Technical Advisory group on monitoring the application of existing treaty Norms for taxing business profits, OECD Report, OECD, Paris, retrieved from www.oecd.org/tax/taxtreaties/35869032.pdf.

OECD (2005), E-Commerce: Transfer Pricing and Business Profits Taxation, OECD Tax Policy Studies, No. 10, OECD, Paris, retrieved from *http://books.google.fr/.*

Annex A

Data on corporate tax revenue as a percentage of GDP

Table A.1. **Corporate tax revenue, % of GDP, 1990-2011**

Country \ Year	1990	1991	1992	1993	1994	1995	1996	1997	1998	1999	2000	2001	2002	2003	2004	2005	2006	2007	2008	2009	2010	2011
Australia	4.0	3.8	3.8	3.4	3.9	4.2	4.3	4.2	4.3	4.6	6.1	4.4	5.0	5.0	5.5	5.8	6.4	6.9	5.9	4.8	4.8	.
Austria	1.4	1.4	1.7	1.5	1.3	1.4	1.9	2.0	2.1	1.8	2.0	3.0	2.2	2.2	2.2	2.2	2.2	2.4	2.5	1.7	1.9	2.2
Belgium	2.0	2.0	1.5	2.0	2.2	2.3	2.7	2.8	3.4	3.2	3.2	3.1	3.0	2.9	3.1	3.3	3.5	3.5	3.3	2.5	2.7	3.0
Canada	2.5	2.1	1.8	2.1	2.5	2.9	3.2	3.8	3.6	4.2	4.4	3.3	3.0	3.2	3.5	3.4	3.8	3.5	3.4	3.4	3.3	3.1
Chile	.	.	.	.	.	.	.	.	.	.	.	.	.	.	.	.	.	.	.	.	.	.
Czech Republic	.	.	.	6.4	5.1	4.4	3.2	3.7	3.3	3.7	3.4	3.9	4.2	4.4	4.4	4.4	4.6	4.7	4.2	3.6	3.4	3.5
Denmark	1.7	1.6	1.8	2.0	2.0	2.3	2.5	2.7	3.0	2.4	3.3	2.8	2.9	2.9	3.2	3.9	4.3	3.8	3.3	2.3	2.7	2.8
Estonia	.	.	.	.	.	2.4	1.6	1.8	2.4	2.0	0.9	0.7	1.1	1.6	1.7	1.4	1.5	1.6	1.6	1.9	1.4	1.3
Finland	2.0	2.0	1.6	0.3	0.6	2.3	2.8	3.5	4.3	4.3	5.9	4.2	4.2	3.4	3.5	3.3	3.4	3.9	3.5	2.0	2.6	2.7
France	2.2	1.9	2.0	1.9	2.0	2.1	2.3	2.6	2.6	3.0	3.1	3.4	2.9	2.5	2.8	2.4	3.0	3.0	2.9	1.5	2.1	2.5
Germany	1.7	1.6	1.5	1.3	1.1	1.0	1.4	1.5	1.6	1.8	1.8	0.6	1.0	1.3	1.6	1.8	2.2	2.2	1.9	1.3	1.5	1.7
Greece	1.5	1.2	1.3	1.4	1.7	1.8	1.8	1.9	2.8	3.2	4.2	3.4	3.4	2.9	3.0	3.3	2.7	2.6	2.5	2.5	2.4	.
Hungary	.	4.6	2.4	1.7	1.9	1.9	1.8	1.9	2.1	2.3	2.2	2.3	2.3	2.2	2.2	2.1	2.3	2.8	2.6	2.3	1.2	1.2
Iceland	0.9	0.8	1.0	0.9	0.7	0.9	0.9	0.9	1.1	1.3	1.2	1.0	0.9	1.2	1.0	2.0	2.4	2.5	1.9	1.8	1.0	1.6
Ireland	1.6	2.0	2.3	2.7	3.0	2.7	3.1	3.1	3.3	3.8	3.7	3.5	3.7	3.7	3.5	3.4	3.7	3.4	2.8	2.4	2.5	2.3
Israel	.	.	.	.	.	3.1	2.9	3.4	3.3	3.0	3.9	3.5	2.8	2.9	3.4	4.0	4.9	4.5	3.5	2.8	2.9	3.7
Italy	3.8	3.7	4.2	3.9	3.6	3.5	3.8	4.1	2.9	3.3	2.9	3.5	3.1	2.8	2.8	2.8	3.4	3.8	3.7	3.1	2.8	2.7
Japan	6.4	5.9	4.8	4.2	4.0	4.2	4.5	4.2	3.7	3.4	3.7	3.5	3.1	3.3	3.7	4.2	4.8	4.8	3.9	2.6	3.2	3.3
Korea	2.5	2.1	2.4	2.1	2.3	2.3	2.3	2.0	2.3	1.8	3.2	2.8	3.0	3.7	3.3	3.8	3.6	4.0	4.2	3.7	3.5	4.0
Luxembourg	5.6	5.1	4.4	5.9	6.0	6.6	6.8	7.5	7.6	6.7	7.0	7.3	8.0	7.3	5.7	5.8	5.0	5.3	5.1	5.6	5.7	5.0
Mexico	.	.	.	.	.	.	.	.	.	.	.	.	.	.	.	.	.	.	.	.	.	..
Netherlands	3.2	3.3	2.9	3.2	3.2	3.1	3.9	4.3	4.2	4.1	4.0	3.9	3.3	2.8	3.1	3.8	3.3	3.2	3.2	2.0	2.2	.
New Zealand	2.4	2.5	3.0	3.6	4.4	4.3	3.3	3.8	3.5	3.7	4.1	3.7	4.2	4.6	5.4	6.1	5.7	4.9	4.4	3.5	3.8	3.9
Norway	3.7	4.0	2.9	3.3	3.4	3.8	4.3	5.1	4.1	4.6	8.9	8.9	8.1	8.0	9.8	11.7	12.8	11.0	12.1	9.1	10.1	11.0
Poland	.	6.7	4.2	3.9	2.9	2.8	2.7	2.7	2.6	2.4	2.4	1.9	2.0	1.8	2.2	2.5	2.4	2.8	2.7	2.3	2.0	.
Portugal	2.1	2.5	2.4	2.0	2.1	2.3	2.7	3.1	3.1	3.5	3.7	3.3	3.3	2.8	2.9	2.7	2.9	3.6	3.7	2.9	2.8	.
Slovak Republic	.	.	.	.	.	6.0	4.3	3.7	3.2	3.1	2.6	2.6	2.5	2.8	2.6	2.7	2.9	3.0	3.1	2.5	2.5	2.6
Slovenia	.	.	.	.	.	0.5	0.9	1.0	1.0	1.2	1.2	1.3	1.6	1.7	1.9	2.8	3.0	3.2	2.5	1.8	1.9	1.7

Country / Year	1990	1991	1992	1993	1994	1995	1996	1997	1998	1999	2000	2001	2002	2003	2004	2005	2006	2007	2008	2009	2010	2011
Spain	2.9	2.5	2.2	1.9	1.6	1.7	1.9	2.6	2.4	2.7	3.1	2.8	3.2	3.1	3.4	3.9	4.1	4.7	2.8	2.2	1.8	1.8
Sweden	1.6	1.7	1.4	2.0	2.5	2.8	2.6	2.9	2.7	2.9	3.9	2.9	2.3	2.4	3.0	3.7	3.6	3.7	3.0	3.0	3.5	3.5
Switzerland	1.8	1.7	1.8	1.7	1.7	1.7	1.7	1.8	1.9	2.3	2.6	2.9	2.5	2.4	2.3	2.4	2.9	3.0	3.1	3.0	2.9	2.9
Turkey	1.0	0.9	0.8	0.8	1.0	1.1	1.1	1.2	1.2	1.8	1.8	1.8	1.8	2.1	1.7	1.7	1.5	1.6	1.8	1.9	1.9	2.1
United Kingdom	3.5	2.8	2.1	1.9	2.2	2.8	3.2	3.8	3.9	3.5	3.5	3.4	2.8	2.7	2.8	3.3	3.9	3.4	3.6	2.8	3.1	2.8
United States	2.4	2.2	2.3	2.5	2.7	2.9	2.9	2.9	2.7	2.7	2.6	1.9	1.7	2.1	2.5	3.2	3.4	3.0	2.0	1.8	2.7	2.6
OECD – Total	2.6	2.7	2.4	2.5	2.5	2.8	2.8	3.0	3.0	3.1	3.4	3.2	3.1	3.1	3.2	3.6	3.8	3.8	3.5	2.8	2.9	.

Notes: · Hungary (1.2): the figures are on a cash basis.

· Ireland (2.3) and Mexico (..): central government and Social Security funds only.

· Japan (3.3): the tax revenue figures exclude revenue for Social Security funds. Figures are not available.

Source: Data extracted on 27 November 2012 from OECD.STAT – data regarding Chile and Mexico are not included as it is not possible to breakdown substantial proportions of their revenues from incomes, profits and gains into personal and corporate.

The statistical data for Israel are supplied by and under the responsibility of the relevant Israeli authorities. The use of such data by the OECD is without prejudice to the status of the Golan Heights, East Jerusalem and Israeli settlements in the West Bank under the terms of international law.

Annex B

A review of recent studies relating to BEPS

There are a number of recent studies analysing the ETRs of MNEs in an attempt to demonstrate the existence of BEPS behaviour, or the absence of such behaviour. In most cases these studies use backward-looking approaches and firm-level data. Some studies, mostly from the United States, used data from taxpayers' returns.[1] Other studies focused on different data, such as investment flows and positions, to investigate the extent of BEPS. The studies and their conclusions are briefly summarised below.[2]

Studies of effective tax rates of MNEs

A recent report (J.P. Morgan, 2012) contrasts the business models of IP-rich MNEs (referred to as Global Tax Rate Makers) with that of companies whose business model is predominately restricted to competing within U.S. borders (referred to as Domestic Tax Rate Takers). According to the report, in aggregate Global Tax Rate Makers show a weighted-average, 10-year, long-term effective tax rate of 22.4% and a simple-average, 10-year, long-term effective tax rate of 22.6%. Domestic Tax Rate Takers show a weighted-average, 10-year, long-term effective tax rate of 36.2% and a simple-average, 10-year, long-term effective tax rate of 36.8%.

A recent study (Avi-Yonah and Lahav, 2011), examines the overall ETRs of the largest 100 United States based multinationals over the period 2001-10 and compares them with the ETRs of the largest 100 EU-based multinationals. The study found that, despite the US statutory corporate tax rate being 10% higher than the average statutory corporate tax rate in the EU, the effective tax rates are comparable and that EU MNEs tend to have a higher ETR (on average approximately 34%) than United States MNEs (on average approximately 30%).

A study by the United States Bureau of Economic Analysis (Yorgason, 2009), based on comprehensive data on United States MNEs collected on a yearly basis between 1982 and 2007, reports that effective average income tax rates borne in the period 2004-07 by United States parent companies (22.8% in 2006) and United States affiliates of non-United States enterprises (28.8% in 2006) are much higher than the average for foreign affiliates (14.6% in 2006).

A National Bureau of Economic Research working paper (Markle and Shackelford, 2011) analysed publicly available data from 28 343 financial statements of 11 602 public corporations from 82 countries from 1988 to 2009 to estimate the trend of country-level ETRs over time. Further, based on data from years 2005 to 2009, the paper tests whether domestic companies (*i.e.* companies operating in only one country) and MNEs face similar ETRs and how ETRs vary across industries. The analysis finds that multinationals and domestic-only firms face similar ETRs and that the evidence mostly shows that the location of the headquarters and the residence of its foreign subsidiaries affects a MNE's global ETR. Specifically, the paper found that the median ETRs for MNEs with headquarters in high-tax countries roughly double those in low-tax countries: MNEs domiciled in Japan face the highest ETRs (median ETRs of 37%), followed by those domiciled in the United States (30%), Australia (26%), France and Germany (25%), while MNEs domiciled in low-tax jurisdictions usually enjoy the lowest ETRs (14%).

There are also a number of studies carried out by campaigners and lobbyists, which reach very different conclusions regarding the level of corporate tax imposed on MNEs. A study recently conducted by Citizens for Tax Justice with the Institute on Taxation and Economic Policy (2011), concludes that the 280 large United States companies chosen from the Fortune 500 List had, on average, an ETR of about 18.5% for the tax years 2008-10, with a quarter of the companies paying effective federal tax rates on their US profits of less than 10% while about the same number paid around 35%. The study asserts that these results are due to incentives contained in the tax code as well as shifting profits into low-tax jurisdictions. Similarly, a study of The Greenlining Institute (2012), on the 30 top tech companies in the United States concludes that the ETR paid by these companies decreased from 23.6% in 2009 to 19.9% in 2010 and 16% in 2011. The study further notes that, at the end of 2009, United States companies had at least USD 1 trillion of foreign retained earnings and considers this as a clear indication of profit shifting practices put in place by United States based MNEs.[3]

On the other hand, a study commissioned by the Business Roundtable carried out by PriceWaterhouseCooper in 2011 reaches different conclusions. The study analyses the ETRs of the 2 000 largest companies in 59 countries for the period 2006-09 and concludes that United States-based companies face an average ETR of 27.7% compared to an average ETR of 19.5% for foreign-based companies included in the analysis. Similarly, research conducted by the American Enterprise Institute for Public Policy Research in 2011, considers investment in plant and equipment, financed by retained earnings. It finds that, in 2010, the United States effective average tax rate was 29%, compared to a 27-nation average of 20.6%, while the United States effective marginal tax rate was 23.6%, with the 27-nation average at 17.3%.

It is questionable whether any of the foregoing studies provide conclusive evidence that BEPS behaviours are prevalent. In fact, none of these studies identifies data specifically related to BEPS and the differences or similarities in ETRs observed in the studies could well be attributable to factors other than BEPS. It is thus difficult to build up an aggregate picture of the scale of BEPS.

Studies using data from taxpayer returns

A recent study (Grubert, 2012), analyses data from a linked sample of 754 large non-financial U.S.-based MNCs obtained from the Treasury corporate income tax files and finds that the share of aggregate pre-tax worldwide income earned abroad increased from 37.1% in 1996 to 51.1% in 2004. This increase in the foreign share of total income was almost completely in the form of income that is not repatriated from abroad, which rose from 17.4% of worldwide income in 1996 to 31.4% in 2004. The study concludes that the differential between domestic and foreign effective tax rates has a significant effect on the share of MNE income abroad. This effect operates mainly through changes in foreign and domestic profit margins rather than changes in the location of sales. Companies with lower effective foreign tax rates have both higher foreign profit margins and lower domestic profit margins. This evidence of income shifting from the United States is supplemented by the finding that increased R&D performed in the United States magnifies the impact of U.S.-foreign tax differentials.

The study considers that problems in pricing intellectual property create greater opportunities for income shifting. The paper also examines the relationship between a company's effective foreign tax rate and its domestic and worldwide growth, and concludes that it is difficult to detect any significant effect of lower foreign tax rates on domestic sales and that lower tax burdens on foreign MNE income do not seem to increase companies' worldwide growth. Accordingly, the evidence for the "competitiveness" benefits of lower taxes on foreign income does not seem very strong.

Another study (McDonald, 2008) updates, modifies, and extends research to investigate income shifting from intercompany transfer pricing via theoretical and regression models developed in previous studies (Grubert, 2003). The models are modified slightly to capture the effects of "real" intercompany tangible, intangible, and services transactions (as opposed to interest "income stripping" through intercompany or inter-branch debt), and extended to incorporate data relating to cost sharing arrangements. The study concludes that while the ability to draw transactional transfer pricing inferences from tax return and cost sharing arrangements data is to some extent limited, the analysis demonstrates that the tax data are consistent with (although do not conclusively prove) the existence of potential income shifting from non-arm's length transfer pricing.

The original study (Grubert, 2003) investigates the links between intangible income, intercompany transactions, income shifting and the choice of location by using data on U.S. parent corporations and their manufacturing subsidiaries. The results of the analysis show that income derived from R&D based intangibles accounts for about half of the income shifted from high-tax to low-tax countries and that R&D intensive subsidiaries engage in a greater volume of intercompany transactions, thus having more opportunities for income shifting. Furthermore, subsidiaries in locations with either very high or very low statutory tax rates, with a strong incentive to shift income in or out, also undertake a significantly larger volume of intercompany transactions. The results also provide evidence of income shifting by R&D intensive U.S. parent companies which invest to very high-tax or very low-tax countries. As a sidelight, the study finds that the allocation of debt among subsidiaries and the shifting of R&D based intangible income together account for virtually all of the observed difference in profitability between high and low-tax countries.

A report by the United States General Accountability Office (2008) analysed Internal Revenue Service data on corporate taxpayers, including new data for 2004 and Bureau of Economic Analysis data on the domestic and foreign operations of United States MNEs. The average United States effective tax rate on the domestic income of large corporations with positive domestic income in 2004 was an estimated 25.2%. There was considerable variation in tax rates across these taxpayers, with about one-third of the taxpayers having effective rates of 10% or less and a quarter of the taxpayers having rates over 50%. The average United States ETR on the foreign-source income of these large corporations was calculated to be around 4%, reflecting the effects of both the foreign tax credit (as the United States only imposes a residual tax on foreign income after crediting foreign taxes paid abroad on that income) and tax deferral (as foreign income is not taxed until repatriated to the United States).

The report also analysed trends in the location of worldwide activity of United States based businesses measured by sales, value added, employment, compensation, physical assets, and net income. United States business activity increased in absolute terms both domestically and abroad from 1989 through 2004, but the relative share of activity that was based in foreign affiliates increased. The report notes that the United Kingdom, Canada, and Germany are the leading foreign locations of United States businesses by all measures except income. According to the report, this is due to the fact that reporting of the geographic sources of income is susceptible to manipulation for tax planning purposes and appears to be influenced by differences in tax rates across countries. This appears to be confirmed by the fact that most of the countries studied with relatively low effective tax rates have income shares significantly larger than their shares of the business measures least likely to be affected by income shifting practice (physical assets, compensation, and employment) while the opposite relationship holds for most of the high tax countries studied.[4]

Other analyses of profit shifting

A recent study (Heckemeyer and Overesch, 2012), provides a quantitative review of the empirical literature on profit shifting behaviour of MNEs. It analyses evidence from 23 studies and finds indirect evidence for profit shifting based on the correlation according to which reported taxable profit is inversely related to the difference between the local tax rate and tax levels at other group locations. Based on its analyses, the study also asserts that that transfer pricing and licensing, not inter-company debt, is the dominant profit shifting channel.

Another study looks specifically at the effects of income-shifting practices of United States based MNEs (Clausing, 2011). Using data from the United States Bureau of Economic Analysis, the study finds large discrepancies between the physical operations of affiliates abroad and the locations in which they report their profits for tax purposes: the top ten locations for affiliate employment (in order: the United Kingdom, Canada, Mexico, China, Germany, France, Brazil, India, Japan, Australia) barely match with the top ten locations for gross profits reporting (in order: the Netherlands, Luxembourg, Ireland, Canada, Bermuda, Switzerland, Singapore, Germany, Norway and Australia).

A report of the United States Congressional Research Service (Gravelle, 2010) concludes that there is ample and clear evidence that profits appear in countries inconsistent with an economic motivation. The report analysed the profits of United States controlled foreign corporations as a percentage of the GDP of the countries in which they are located. It finds that for the G-7 countries the ratio ranges from 0.2% to 2.6% (in the case of Canada). The ratio is equal to 4.6% for the Netherlands, 7.6% for Ireland, 9.8% for Cyprus, 18.2% for Luxembourg. Finally, the study notes that the ratio increases dramatically for no-tax jurisdictions with for example, 35.3% for Jersey, 43.3% for Bahamas, 61.1% for Liberia, 354.6% for British Virgin Islands, 546.7% for the Cayman Islands and 645.7% for Bermuda.

Focusing on the behaviour of European MNEs, a study conducted by European Commission staff (Huizinga and Laeven, 2006), found that significant international tax rate differences provide European MNEs powerful incentives to re-allocate profits internationally. It analysed a dataset containing detailed firm-level information on the parent companies and subsidiaries of European multinationals from the Amadeus database, coupled with information about international tax rates. The study suggests that international profit shifting by an individual MNE depends on its international structure and on the international tax regime it faces in each of the countries in which it operates. According to this study, the costs of international profit shifting are considerable and profit shifting leads to a significant redistribution of national corporate tax revenues in Europe.

Another study (Weichenrieder, 2006), attempted to identify profit shifting behaviour looking at the correlation between the home country tax rate of a parent and the net of tax profitability of its German subsidiary, using 116 632 firm-year observations during the period 1996-2003. The study concludes that for profitable subsidiaries that are directly owned by a foreign investor, the evidence suggests that a 10 percentage point increase in the parent's home country tax rate leads to roughly half a percentage point increase in the profitability of the German subsidiary. This is based on the assumption that the lower the tax rate of a foreign parent is vis-à-vis the rate that is applicable to its German affiliate, the more profitable it will be to shift the profits of the affiliate to the home country of the parent.

Another study (Dischinger, 2012) concludes that there is indirect empirical evidence of profit shifting by MNEs out of the European Union. Profit shifting behaviour is analysed in a panel study for the years 1995 to 2005 using a large micro database of European subsidiaries of MNEs which includes detailed balance sheet items. The study finds a decrease in the unconsolidated pre-tax profits of an affiliated company of approximately 7% if the difference in the statutory corporate tax rate of this affiliate to its parent increases by 10%, thus suggesting an overall shift of profits out of the European Union. Further, the study also notes that a higher parent's ownership share of its subsidiary leads to intensified profit shifting behaviour.

Similar results emerge from studies using different methodologies to estimate the existence and magnitude of tax-motivated income shifting within MNEs. A recent study (Dharmapala, D. and Riedel N., 2012), exploits exogenous earnings increases at the parent firm and investigates how these increased profits propagate across low-tax and high-tax entities within the MNE group. The study applies this approach to a panel of European MNE's affiliates over the period 1995-2005 and concludes that parents' positive earnings shocks are associated with a significantly positive increase in pre-tax profits at low-tax affiliates, relative to the effect on the pre-tax profits of high-tax affiliates. On the basis of additional tests, the study suggests that this estimated effect is attributable primarily to the strategic use of debt across affiliates.

There are also a few studies focusing on developing countries. A report prepared for the UK Department for International Development analysed existing literature on the tax gap suffered by developing countries due to tax avoidance and tax evasion (Fuest and Riedel, 2009). The report concludes that the available knowledge on tax revenue loss in developing countries caused by tax evasion and tax avoidance is very limited. This is partly due to the lack of data and partly due to methodological shortcomings of existing studies (*e.g.* impossibility of disentangle quality differences and income shifting when analysing international trade mispricing; way in which estimates of mispricing are translated into tax revenue losses). The report concludes that more research is needed to understand to improve the understanding of tax avoidance and evasion and their implications for revenue mobilisation in developing countries.

A subsequent study from the same authors (Fuest, and Riedel, 2010) reiterates that the results of many existing studies on tax avoidance and evasion in developing countries are difficult to interpret, mainly because the measurement concepts used have a number of drawbacks, face methodological difficulties and rely on a number of strong assumptions. The study then discusses alternative methods and suggests the use of datasets such as ORBIS, COMPUSTAT, the BEA Database on Operations of Multinational Companies, the UK Office of National Statistics Annual Inquiry into Foreign Direct Investment (AFDI) and the Deutsche Bundesbank Microdatabase on Direct Investments (MiDi), recommending micro data sources as better suited to identify corporate profit shifting activities. Finally, the study presents some empirical evidence which supports the view that profit shifting out of many developing countries and into tax havens does indeed take place.

Notes

1. It should be noted that the disproportionate analyses of U.S.-based multinationals summarised in this section are solely a reflection of the relatively high quality and availability of such data.

2. There are also a number of earlier studies which have addressed the issue of BEPS and which are not summarised here. These include: Grubert, H. and Mutti, J.,

Taxes, Tariffs and Transfer Pricing in Multinational Corporate Decision Making, The Review of Economics and Statistics, Vol. 73, No. 2 (May, 1991), pp. 285-293; Harris, D.G., *The Impact of U.S. Tax Law Revision on Multinational Corporations' Capital Location and Income-Shifting Decisions,* Journal of Accounting Research, Vol. 31, Studies on International Accounting (1993), pp. 111-140; Jacob, J., *Taxes and Transfer Pricing: Income Shifting and the Volume of Intrafirm Transfers,* Journal of Accounting Research, Vol. 34, No. 2 (Autumn, 1996), pp. 301-312; Rousslang, D.J., *International income shifting by US multinational corporations,* Applied Economics, Vol. 29, No. 7 (1997), pp. 925-934; Altshuler, R., Grubert, H. and Newlon, T.S., *Has U.S. Investment Abroad Become More Sensitive to Tax Rates?,* NBER Working Paper Series, Working Paper No. 6383, January 1998; Grubert, H., *Taxes and the division of foreign operating income among royalties, interest, dividends and retained earnings*, Journal of Public Economics, Vol. 68 (1998), pp. 269–290; Gorter, J. and de Mooij, R.A., *Capital Income Taxation in Europe. Trends and trade-offs*, CPB Netherlands Bureau for Economic Policy Analysis, Special Publication No. 30 (May 2001); Collins, J.H. and Shackelford, D.A, *Do U.S. Multinationals Face Different Tax Burdens than Other Companies?*, NBER, Tax Policy and the Economy, Vol. 17 (January 2003); De Mooij, R.A. and Ederveen, S., *Taxation and Foreign Direct Investment: A Synthesis of Empirical Research,* International Tax and Public Finance, Vol. 10, pp. 673–693 (2003); Desai, M.A., Foley, F. and Hines J.R., *A Multinational Perspective on Capital Structure Choice and Internal Capital Markets*, The Journal of Finance, Vol. 59, No. 6 (December 2004).

3. The amount is reported to be 1.7 trillion USD at the end of 2011. See Morgan, J.P. (2012), *Global Tax Rate Makers: Undistributed Foreign Earnings Top $1.7 Trillion; At least 60% of Multinational Cash is Abroad.*

4. The comparisons summarised in this paragraph rely on accounting and tax return data. Because intangible development costs are often expensed, the business activity comparisons may therefore not always reflect intangible assets held in low-tax jurisdictions. One important profit shifting issue is whether proper payments are made in transferring the intangibles to the low-tax countries, a topic not directly addressed by the comparison of income and assets / business activity based on accounting information. As a result, the available data may not be fully adequate to precisely answer the relevant question of whether unjustified profit shifting exists.

Bibliography

American Enterprise Institute for Public Policy Research (2011), *Report Card on Effective Corporate Tax Rates: United States Gets an F*, Tax Policy Outlook No. 1, February 2011. Retrieved from *www.aei.org/files/2011/02/09/TPO-2011-01-g.pdf*.

Avi-Yonah, R. and Y. Lahav (2011), *The Effective Tax Rate of the Largest US and EU Multinationals*, University of Michigan Law School, Program in Law & Economics, Working Paper No. 41. Retrieved from *http://law.bepress.com/cgi/viewcontent.cgi?article=1150&context=umichlwps-empirical*.

Citizens for Tax Justice with the Institute on Taxation and Economic Policy (2011), *Corporate Taxpayers and Corporate Tax Dodgers 2008-10*, November 2011. Retrieved from *www.ctj.org/corporatetaxdodgers/CorporateTaxDodgersReport.pdf*.

Clausing, K.A. (2011), *The Revenue Effects of Multinational Firm Income Shifting*, Tax Notes, 28 March 2011, pp. 1580-1586.

Dharmapala, D. and N. Riedel. (2013), *Earnings Shocks and Tax-Motivated Income-Shifting: Evidence from European Multinationals*, CESifo Working Paper, Public Finance, No. 3791, Journal of Public Economics, Vol. 97, January 2013, pp. 95-107.

Dischinger, M. (2007), *Profit Shifting by Multinationals: Indirect Evidence from European Micro Data*, Munich Discussion Paper No. 2007-30, University of Munich, Department of Economics, 15 September 2007.

Fuest, C. and N. Riedel (2009), *Tax Evasion, Tax Avoidance and Tax Expenditures in Developing Countries: a Review of the Literature*, Report prepared for the UK Department for International Development (DFID), 19 June 2009. Retrieved from *www.dfid.gov.uk/r4d/PDF/Outputs/EcoDev/60670_TaxEvasionReportDFIDFINAL1906.pdf*.

Fuest, C. and N. Riedel. (2010), *Tax Evasion and Tax Avoidance in Developing Countries: the Role of International Profit Shifting,* Oxford University Centre for Business Taxation, Working Paper 10/12, June 2010. Retrieved from *www.sbs.ox.ac.uk/centres/tax/Documents/working_papers/WP1012.pdf*.

Gravelle, J.G. (2010), *Tax Havens: International Tax Avoidance and Evasion*, United States Congressional Research Service, CRS Report for Congress, 3 September 2010. Retrieved from *www.fas.org/sgp/crs/misc/R40623.pdf*.

The Greenlining Institute (2012), *Tech Untaxed – Tax Avoidance in Silicon Valley, and How America's Richest Company Pays a Lower Tax Rate than You Do*, April 2012. Retrieved from *http://greenlining.org/resources/pdfs/TechUntaxedReport.pdf.*

Grubert, H. (2012), *Foreign Taxes and the Growing Share of U.S. Multination Company Income Abroad: Profits, Not Sales, Are Being Globalized*, Office of Tax Analysis Working Paper No. 103, February 2012. Retrieved from *www.treasury.gov/resource-center/tax-policy/tax-analysis/Documents/OTA-W2012-103-Multinational-Income-Globalized-Feb-2012.pdf.*

Grubert, H. (2003), *Intangible Income, Intercompany Transactions, Income Shifting, and the Choice of Location,* National Tax Journal, Vol. 56, No. 1, Part 2, March 2003, pp. 221-242.

Heckemeyer, J. and M. Overesch (2012), *Profit Shifting Channels of Multinational Firms – a Meta Study*, paper presented at IIPF Congress August 2012. Retrieved from *http://editorialexpress.com/cgi-bin/conference/download.cgi?db_name=IIPF68&paper_id=434.*

Huizinga, H. and L. Laeven (2006), *International profit shifting within multinationals: A multi-country perspective*, Economic Papers No. 260 December 2006. Retrieved from *http://ec.europa.eu/economy_finance/publications/publication590_en.pdf.*

J.P. Morgan (2012), North America Equity Research, *Global Tax Rate Makers: Undistributed Foreign Earnings Top $1.7 Trillion; At least 60% of Multinational Cash is Abroad*, 16 May 2012.

Markle, K.S. and D.A. Hackelford (2011), *Cross-country Comparisons of corporate income taxes*, National Bureau of Economic Research Working Paper No. 16839, February 2011.

McDonald, M. (2008), *Income Shifting from Transfer Pricing: Further Evidence from Tax Return Data*, Office of Tax Analysis, OTA Technical Working Paper 2, July 2008. Retrieved from *www.treasury.gov/resource-center/tax-policy/ta x-analysis/documents/otatech02.pdf.*

PwC (2011), *Global Effective Tax Rates*, 14 April 2011. Retrieved from *http://businessroundtable.org/uploads/studies-reports/downloads/Effective_Tax_Rate_Study.pdf.*

United States General Accountability Office (2008), *US Multinational Corporations – ETRs Are Correlated with Where Income Is Reported*, August 2008. Retrieved from *www.gao.gov/new.items/d08950.pdf.*

Weichenrieder, A. (2006), *Profit Shifting in the EU – Evidence from Germany*, University of Frankfurt & CESifo, 7 April 2006. Retrieved from *www.ifs.org.uk/conferences/etpf_weichenreider.pdf*.

Yorgason, D.R. (2009), *Collection of data on income and other taxes in surveys of U.S. multinational enterprises*, Bureau of Economic Analysis Paper prepared for the 4th Joint Session of the Working Group on International Investment Statistics, 8 October 2009. Retrieved from *www.bea.gov/papers/pdf/Yorgason_multinational_taxes.pdf*.

Annex C

Examples of MNEs' tax planning structures

In practice any international tax planning will need to incorporate a number of co-ordinated strategies, which often can be broken down into four elements:

- **Minimisation of taxation in a foreign operating or source country** (which is often a medium to high tax jurisdiction) either by shifting gross profits via trading structures or reducing net profit by maximising deductions at the level of the payer;
- **Low or no withholding tax at source**;
- **Low or no taxation at the level of the recipient** (which can be achieved via low-tax jurisdictions, preferential regimes or hybrid mismatch arrangements) with entitlement to substantial non-routine profits often built up via intra-group arrangements; and
- **No current taxation of the low-taxed profits** (achieved via the first three steps) at the level of the ultimate parent.

Further, effective cash repatriation strategies may be an issue where for instance, dividends need to be funded and of course, "permanent" foreign re-investment of low-taxed cash will be relevant to allow booking of a particular tax rate for EPS purposes.

Any analysis of BEPS therefore needs to be cognizant of the inter-connection of these elements and the overall drivers of the tax planning strategy. The structures described in this annex have been given wide coverage in the specialised and mainstream press. They have been selected because they encapsulate a number of the corporate tax planning opportunities described above and all appear to be perfectly legal under the tax systems of the countries in which they have been put in place. They may therefore constitute a useful paradigm to identify key pressure areas from a tax policy perspective.

E-commerce structure using a two-tiered structure and transfer of intangibles under a cost-contribution arrangement

Company A is a company that is organised in Country A and that initially developed technology and intangibles supporting its business through research conducted primarily in Country A. Company A is the parent of a multinational group of companies.

Under the tax planning structure of the Group, rights to technology developed by the parent, Company A, are licenced or otherwise transferred to Company C under a cost sharing or cost contribution arrangement. Company C is an unlimited liability company organised (*i.e.* registered) under the laws of Country B but managed and controlled in Country C, and so tax resident in Country C. Under the cost sharing arrangement, Company C agrees to make a "buy in" payment equal to the value of the existing technology transferred under the arrangement and to share the cost of future enhancement of the transferred technology. The buy-in payment would be fully taxable in Country A and could take the form of a single lump-sum payment or a running royalty over time. Ongoing research expense would be shared on the basis of the relative anticipated benefits from the intangibles being developed. The cost sharing arrangement would typically be established early in the life of Company A, before development of a significant track record of sales in the markets allocated to Company C under the agreement.[1]

Company C licences all of its rights in the technology to Company D in exchange for a running royalty. Company D is a company organised, managed and controlled in Country D. Company D in turn sub-licences the technology to Company B.

Figure C.1. **Group A's tax-planning structure**

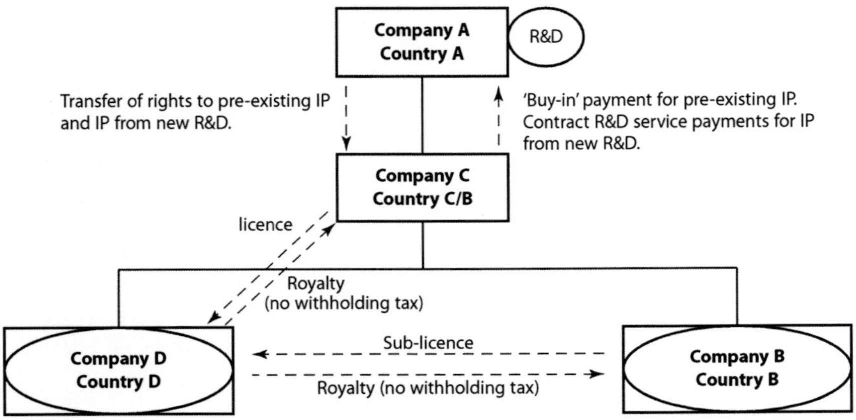

Source: OECD.

Company B is organised, managed and controlled in Country B. Company B employs several thousand people in its operations in Country B. Country B imposes corporate income tax on taxable profit of Company B. However, the taxable profit of Company B is less than 1 per cent of its gross revenues. This is because in calculating its income in Country B, following the OECD transfer pricing principles Company B deducts the full amount of the royalty it pays to Company D for the search and advertising technology.

The royalty payment made by Company B to Company D is free of withholding tax in Country B. Country B would impose a withholding tax on payments directly to a company tax resident in a country like Country C. However, under the law of Country B, applying the EU Interest and Royalties Directive, because the royalty payments are made to a company which is organised and subject to tax in a country that is a member of the European Union, the royalties qualify for exemption from Country B withholding tax.

Country D imposes corporate income tax on the profits of Company D. However, taxable profit is reduced by the deductible royalty payments made by Company D to Company C. Accordingly, corporate income tax is imposed in Country D only on the small amount of royalty "spread" between Company D's royalty receipts from Company B and its royalty payments to Company C. The spread between royalty receipts and royalty payments is very small because Company D engages only in a flow-through transaction. Company D, unlike Company B, performs no functions and holds no assets. It also bears little or no risk with regard to the royalty flows. Under the arm's length principle, it is therefore entitled to very little income. Typically a tax ruling would be obtained in Country D defining the amount of income subject to tax in Country D, thereby providing Group A with certainty regarding the results of its tax planning structure.

Country D does not levy withholding tax on royalty payments under its domestic law. The payments made by Company D to Company C are, therefore, not subject to withholding tax in Country D.

Company C is managed and controlled in Country C. Country C does not impose a corporate income tax. Country B does not impose tax on Company C because it has no presence in Country B, is centrally managed and controlled in Country C and its income arises from sources outside of Country B. Accordingly, the royalty income received by Company C is not subjected to tax in Country D, Country C or Country B.

Under some circumstances, Country A's CFC rules might tax royalty payments received by either Company D or Company C as passive income. However, it is probable that Company A will file a check-the-box election with respect to Company D and Company B. Under such an election, these companies would be disregarded for Country A tax purposes, and the income of Company B and Company D would be treated as having been earned directly by Company C. The royalty transactions between the disregarded entities would similarly be disregarded, meaning that they would be deemed not to exist for Country A tax purposes. For purposes of applying the Country A CFC rules, Company C would therefore be treated as if it had earned the fees and revenues directly through active business operations. Such active business income could be structured in such a way that it would not be subject to tax under the Country A CFC regime.

Transfer of manufacturing operations together with a transfer of supporting intangibles under a cost-contribution arrangement

Company A is a publicly-traded company, based in Country A. It is the parent of an MNE group with global operations. The Group invests heavily in research, product design, and development activities (see Figure C.2).[2] R&D activities are carried out by the parent company, Company A. Previously, Company A owned all IP resulting from its research and development activities. It also had sole responsibility for and risks associated with the manufacture of products and sold those products through a network of sales and distribution companies in markets around the world. Company A's managers then decided to create a wholly-owned subsidiary, Company B in Country B, and assign to it IP and responsibility for the manufacture and sale of products outside of Country A. Company A retained domestic intangible property rights related to the manufacture and sale of products within Country A, and continued to carry out research and development activities for the Group.

At the same time Company B was organised, the Group organised two additional foreign subsidiaries. Each of these companies was wholly-owned by Company B.[3] One of these, Company C, was organised in Country C and serves as the principal company responsible for the manufacture and sale of Group products outside Company A. The other, Company D, is a manufacturing entity responsible for the production of Group products outside of Country A.

While Company C and Company D are treated as corporations under the laws of Country C and Country D, respectively, both are treated as disregarded entities under Country A's check-the-box rules. This treatment carries important implications. Transactions between these disregarded entities and Company B – including royalty and dividend payments to Company B – are disregarded for Country A tax purposes (*i.e.* they are viewed as transactions occurring within the same entity). Moreover, under the check-the-box election, Company B is viewed for Country A tax purposes as performing the activities in fact performed by Company C and Company D.

Figure C.2. **Group A's tax-planning structure**

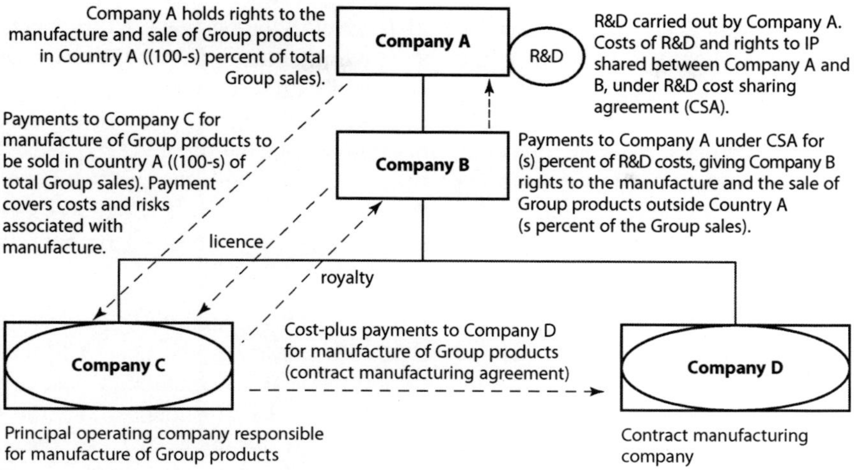

Source: Based on "Present Law and Background Related to Possible Income Shifting and Transfer Pricing", prepared by staff of the Joint Committee on Taxation, submitted to the US House Committee on Ways and Means, 20 July 2010, JCX-37-10, p.93.

The transfer of IP from Company A to Company B is taxable in Country A. Often, but not invariably, in structures of this type the transfer would take place pursuant to a cost-sharing agreement (CSA). Under the CSA, Company C is obliged to make a buy-in payment for pre-existing IP to Company A. The buy-in payment may be structured as either a lump-sum payment or a running royalty. Company C then assumes responsibility going forward to reimburse Company A for a share of ongoing research and development expense reflecting the share of anticipated benefit Company C expects to derive from the ongoing research and development expenditures. For example, if Company C were to be responsible for 45% of global revenues and to derive 45% of global operating income, it would be expected to reimburse Company A for approximately 45% of the product area research and development costs covered under the cost sharing agreement. This effectively eliminates the current Country A tax deduction for that portion of research and development expense reimbursed by Company C under the cost sharing agreement. Despite the fact that Company C reimburses it for a percentage share of its research and development costs, Company A is entitled to an R&D tax credit in Country A for the full amount of its R&D expenditures (including the portion reimbursed by Company B).

By virtue of its buy-in payments and CSA payments, Company B is treated as the owner of the non-Country A IP rights of the Group. Company B licences those IP rights to Company C. Company C contractually assumes responsibility for producing and selling Group products outside Country A and contractually assumes the risks associated with the business. Company C engages Company D to serve as a contract manufacturer. Under the contract manufacturing agreement, Company D manufactures Group products for a fee equal to direct and indirect costs of production plus a 5% mark-up. The manufacturing agreement between Company C and Company D specifies that Company C bears the principal risks associated with the production of the product. Actual production of products may take place in Country D or in a branch of Company D in a low-cost manufacturing country. Company D includes this fee in its taxable income.

The manufactured products are the property of Company C, which sells the products to or through related sales and marketing entities in higher tax jurisdictions around the world. The contractual arrangements between Company C and the marketing companies specify that Company C assumes the principal risks related to the marketing of the products. On this basis, sales and marketing companies are compensated for their efforts on a basis reflecting their limited risk status. Such compensation would usually be computed on the basis of a target return on sales determined for transfer pricing purposes by reference to the returns earned by arguably comparable limited risk marketing and distribution companies. Company C would earn profit equal to its gross sales revenue on foreign sales, less fees paid to Company D for the manufacture of the goods, payments to any related commission-based marketing entities, and less in royalties paid to Company B. This profit is subject to corporate income tax in Country C.

Royalties paid to Company B by Company C for its foreign IP rights are deductible in the computation of the corporate tax base of Company C.[4] As Country C does not impose withholding tax on royalty payments, and Country B does not impose corporate income tax, the royalty is free of withholding tax upon payment, and free of income tax upon receipt. Moreover, possible Country A taxation of Company A on royalty income received by Company B under Country A CFC rules is avoided with application of check-the-box rules under which Company C can be treated as a disregarded entity. Under check-the-box provisions in the Country A, Company C is treated for Country A tax purposes as a branch of Company B. Thus royalty payments from Country C to Company B are treated as payments within a single corporation, and thus are disregarded (not recognised) for Country A tax purposes. Allowing check-the-box provisions to apply in this way effectively allows the Group to erode the Country C tax base with deductible royalty payments and simultaneously side-step application of the Country A CFC provisions that would otherwise apply to royalty income passively received by Company B.

Similarly, dividends paid to Company B are free of tax at source, Country B does not tax dividend income, and the dividend payments are disregarded for Country A tax purposes.

Leveraged acquisition with debt-push down and use of intermediate holding companies

A MNE headquartered in State P and with operations in a number of countries, including State L, plans to acquire a successful manufacturing company resident in State T (Target Co). The acquisition price is EUR 1 billion and about 60% of that will be financed with external bank debt. The remaining 40% will be financed through the MNE's retained earnings.

In order to carry out the acquisition, the MNE sets up a holding company in State L (L Hold Co) which receives an intra-group loan for EUR 400 million. L Hold Co in turn sets up a company in State T (T Hold Co). T Hold Co is financed partly by L Hold Co through a hybrid instrument (EUR 400 million) and partly with the external bank debt (EUR 600 million). T Hold Co acquires Target Co and enters into a tax grouping with the latter for State T tax purposes.

The structure can be depicted as shown in Figure C.3.

Figure C.3. **Leveraged acquisition**

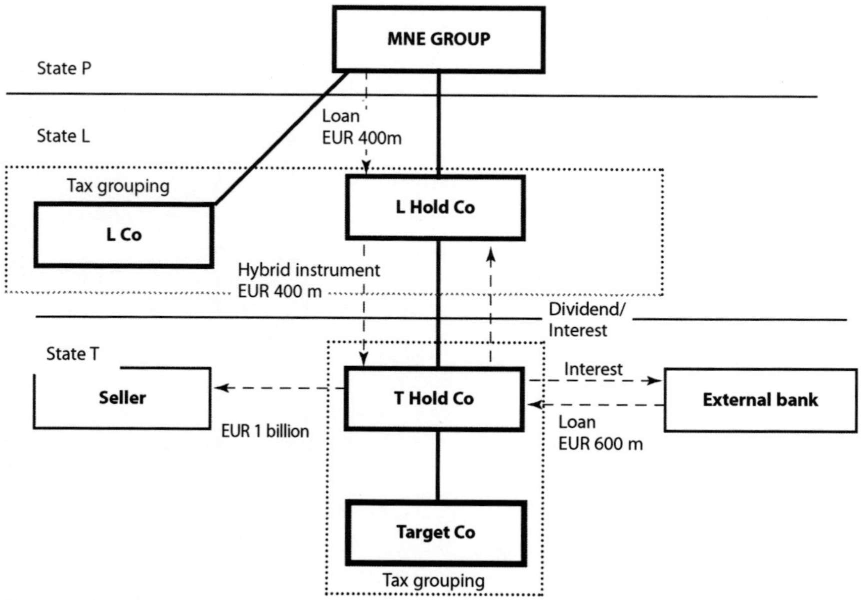

Source: OECD.

This structure potentially allows the MNE group to achieve a number of tax benefits.

The debt push-down technique ensures that subject to applicable limitations interest expenses on the external bank loan are deducted from the target company's operating income through the applicable group tax regimes. L Hold Co finances T Hold Co through a hybrid instrument, *e.g.* redeemable preference shares. This financing is treated as debt in State T while it is treated as equity in State L. As a consequence, and subject to the applicable limitations, additional interest income will be deducted against the income of Target Co for tax purposes. At the same time, the payment will be treated as a dividend and therefore exempt under the domestic law of State L.

Further, the interest L Hold Co pays on the EUR 400 million intra-group loan can also be deducted against the income of other group companies operating in State L (subject to the applicable limitations) via the local tax grouping regime, thus also reducing the tax burden in State L.

The structure also allows the group to claim the benefits of the tax treaty between State T and State L, eliminating or reducing State T withholding tax on the payments made by T Hold Co to L Hold Co.

Upon exiting the investment, the shares in T Hold Co can be sold tax-free to the purchaser. State T may in fact be prevented from taxing the income under the relevant double tax treaty, while State L exempts capital gains on shares under its domestic law.

Notes

1. In the case of Company A and Company C, the arm's length nature of the initial buy-in payment and the formula for sharing future technology development costs was confirmed through an Advance Pricing Agreement, although subsequent changes in Country A law and policy might well make it more difficult to obtain such an APA today.

2. Figure C.2 depicts a simplified version of Company A's Group global structure. Company A, for example, refers to the Country A parent company together with its domestic affiliates (filing a consolidated income tax return).

3. Company B serves in a dual capacity. First, it acts as a holding company for the non-Country A IP rights of the Group. Second, it acts as a holding company for the investments in the shares of Company C and Company D.

4. The royalty payment to Company B may be determined annually under an advanced pricing agreement (APA) or other ruling between Company C and Country C tax authorities. The APA or ruling may stipulate a certain amount of taxable income in Country C determined on the basis of the activities Company C performs and the production risks it takes in Country C. The royalty amount is the residual computed after such taxable returns.

Annex D

Current and past OECD work related to base erosion and profit shifting

For years the OECD has promoted dialogue and co-operation between governments on tax matters. The Model Tax Convention forms the basis for negotiation of existing bilateral tax treaties. The Transfer Pricing Guidelines embody the international standard to allocate profits among different parts of an MNE group. The work on aggressive tax planning helps participating governments to respond more quickly to tax risks. The Forum on Harmful Tax Practices has built support for fair competition with more than 40 potentially harmful member country regimes abolished or modified. The work on tax policy and statistics has dealt with the effects of taxation on FDIs and with how to implement growth-friendly corporate tax reforms. The work on tax administration contributes to improving taxpayer services and tax compliance. The work on tax and development helps developing economies countries in their efforts to mobilise domestic resources. Current and past OECD projects which are directly relevant for BEPS are briefly outlined below in relation to each relevant area of work.

Tax transparency

The current and past work on exchange of information in tax matters has contributed to the unprecedented progress made in this area, with the inclusion of all jurisdictions in the expanding network of international co-operation. This provides increased opportunities to obtain better and more accurate information on BEPS instances that in the past were often not available. In fact, in many cases it would be extremely difficult, if not impossible, to understand the mechanics of certain structures without international co-operation.

Tax treaties

Current work relevant to BEPS includes ongoing work on the definition of permanent establishment, which deals with a number of permanent establishment issues that were raised in the context of the work on business restructurings. It also includes the work on tax treaty issues related to hybrid mismatch arrangements and, in particular, the discussion of a proposal dealing with payments by hybrid entities and the examination of the use of treaty switch-over provisions by exemption countries. The current work on the meaning of beneficial owner, which is nearing completion, is also relevant, primarily as it allowed a greater understanding of the limits of this concept in addressing treaty shopping concerns.

Past work relevant to BEPS includes work on restricting the entitlement to treaty benefits and the abuse of tax treaties which was done between 1998 and 2003, as a follow-up to the 1998 Report on Harmful Tax Competition. That work dealt with various treaty questions related to tax avoidance, including the definition of residence, the concept of beneficial owner, the possible inclusion of specific anti-abuse rules in tax treaties and the interaction between tax treaties and domestic CFC rules, specific anti-abuse rules, GAARs and similar rules and judicial doctrines.[1] Also relevant is the work done between 1998 and 2004 on tax treaty aspects of electronic commerce, and in particular work on the concept of place of effective management and on whether the current rules for taxing business profits were appropriate for electronic commerce.[2]

Transfer pricing

Current work relevant to BEPS includes that on *(i)* intangibles, which seeks to clarify transfer pricing rules related to the use and transfer of intangibles and to clarify the economic substance requirements for taxpayer arrangements to be respected, *(ii)* documentation requirements, which seeks to simplify compliance while simultaneously providing governments with more useful information to evaluate transfer pricing risk, and *(iii)* safe harbour provisions, which seeks to develop mechanisms for resolving less contentious transfer pricing matters efficiently, so that more attention can be given to challenging BEPS-related matters.

Recent work relevant to BEPS includes that on *(i)* business restructuring, which addresses the transfer pricing aspects of corporate restructurings, and in particular addresses for the first time questions related to allocation of risk, *(ii)* profit methods which resulted in new guidance on the selection of the most appropriate transfer pricing method to the circumstances of the case, and the practical application of transactional profit methods, and *(iii)* attribution of profits to permanent establishments, which addresses issues related to the attribution of income to branch operations on a basis consistent with the arm's length principle.

Aggressive tax planning

Current work relevant to BEPS includes that on cross-border acquisition and disposals, which deals with ATP schemes encountered by participating countries in this area, as well as their detection and response strategies. Issues being addressed include: debt-push down, artificial interest deduction techniques, avoidance of withholding tax at source, and circumvention of CFC and thin capitalisation rules. Also relevant is the work on after-tax hedging, which deals with schemes that use the different tax treatment of certain items of income to hedge against a risk on an after-tax basis, and in some cases also enable the taxpayer to obtain additional tax benefits.

Recent work relevant to BEPS includes that on *(i)* hybrid mismatch arrangements, which produces a comprehensive picture of how hybrids are used by taxpayers to achieve unintended mismatches across different countries and recommends countries concerned with these issues to introduce rules linking the tax treatment in their jurisdiction to the one applicable in the other jurisdiction; *(ii)* corporate and bank losses, which identifies key risk areas and describes ATP schemes in this area and recommends countries to introduce or tighten anti-loss trafficking rules; *(iii)* disclosure initiatives, which covers a range of approaches from mandatory disclosure rules to forms of co-operative compliance and recommends countries to consider their introduction or revision; and *(iv)* the ongoing work on schemes posted on aggressive tax planning directory.

Harmful tax practices

Current work relevant to BEPS includes the ongoing review of preferential tax regimes in member countries. The review focuses on regimes which apply to globally mobile activities, such as financial and other service activities, including the provision of intangibles. This review has been the main focus of the FHTP's work since late 2010 and is based upon principles and factors set out in the 1998 Report *Harmful Tax Competition: An Emerging Global Issue.*

Tax policy analyses and statistics

Current work includes the contribution to the OECD horizontal project *New Sources of Growth* (NSG) with a model to measure ETRs on investment in R&D, and in production using knowledge capital generated by that R&D. The model has been constructed to incorporate a range of cross-border tax planning strategies. The OECD-wide report on NSG will use this modelling of ETR to draw some preliminary policy conclusions about what approaches to encouraging investment in knowledge-based assets are likely to be most cost-effective and where there may be unwanted effects in terms of lost tax revenues, economic efficiency losses, distortions of competition.

Recent work includes the report *Tax Effects on Foreign Direct Investment: Recent Evidence and Policy Analysis* (OECD, 2008), which examines empirical studies and models to identify which factors explain differences in the responsiveness of FDI to taxation. Importantly, it addresses considerations in the design of rules governing the taxation of inbound and outbound FDI, including increasing pressure to provide "internationally competitive" tax treatment. Finally, it analyses the implications of tax planning by MNEs in reducing ETRs on cross-border investment (which then resulted in the current work described above). The report *Fundamental Reform of Corporate Income Tax* (OECD, 2007) presents trends in the taxation of corporate income in OECD countries and discusses the main drivers of corporate income tax reform and evaluates the gains of fundamental corporate tax reform. The corporate tax-induced distortions are discussed from a domestic and international tax point of view, taking into account tax revenue and tax complexity issues.

Tax administration

Current work relevant to BEPS includes the Forum on Tax Administration's project to review enhanced relationships with large business, which deals with the impact of co-operative compliance strategies on the behaviour of MNEs and the tangible results in terms of reduced costs for businesses and tax administrations and of improvements in compliance, including the implications for ATP. Other relevant work includes the large business network pilot project on ways to better understand where MNEs are recognising their profits, which aims to understand what ETRs are being paid by MNEs and how closely correlated the reporting of profits is with indicators of the location of the value adding activities that give rise to those profits.

Tax and development

Current work relevant to BEPS includes programmes in a number of countries to provide support on policy issues, administrative structures, regulations and guidance and building practical auditing skills in relation to international tax issues. The programmes also aim to build capacity of developing countries to effectively employ other tools that are available to counter BEPS. Recent work relevant to BEPS includes a study on the potential transparency benefits from the public registration of statutory accounts of unlisted companies particularly for developing countries. Further details are included in Box D.1.

Box D.1. BEPS and developing countries

Improved global rules will only partially address the challenges faced by many developing countries as in such countries there are additional problems to be taken into account. According to OECD Secretariat estimates, the capacity to deal with international tax matters lags significantly behind in up to 54 countries. To enable developing countries to effectively address BEPS issues there is a need for a more coherent and structured approach to providing the support developing countries need to build their capacity to understand and effectively implement international standards aimed at dealing with BEPS issues. Developing countries often have no rules or ineffective rules for dealing with BEPS issues and lack the capacity to draft effective rules. They also face significant challenges in obtaining the relevant data and information to enable them to effectively implement their rules. The other major challenge facing developing countries is building the capacity to effectively implement rules based on international standards. There is already a significant amount of work being done by the OECD and other international organisations to support developing countries to address these challenges. This work aims at disseminating effective international standards, improving access to data and information, building capacity and assisting in tax audits.

Tax Inspectors without Borders (TIWB)

The OECD Task Force on Tax and Development is carrying out a feasibility study to consider options for an international infrastructure to share tax auditing expertise with the aim of enabling developing countries to collect the right amount of tax due to them. TIWB was born from an increased awareness both within and outside the Task Force on Tax and Development of the pressing need to support developing country audit programmes. The proposal builds on the experience of the Task Force's developing country members, some of whom are currently benefitting from the assistance of more experienced tax administrations on a bilateral and ad hoc basis, or which have developed similar broad initiatives in other, related policy areas.

Notes

1. The Secretariat has been directly involved in the recent inclusion, in the UN Model, of some of the results of that work.

2. See the 2004 report "Are the Current Treaty Rules for Taxing Business Profits Appropriate for E-Commerce?" (OECD, 2004) and, in particular, the conclusion, in paragraph 353 of that Report, that "there is a need to continue to monitor how direct tax revenues are affected by changes to business models resulting from new communication technologies".

ORGANISATION FOR ECONOMIC CO-OPERATION AND DEVELOPMENT

The OECD is a unique forum where governments work together to address the economic, social and environmental challenges of globalisation. The OECD is also at the forefront of efforts to understand and to help governments respond to new developments and concerns, such as corporate governance, the information economy and the challenges of an ageing population. The Organisation provides a setting where governments can compare policy experiences, seek answers to common problems, identify good practice and work to co-ordinate domestic and international policies.

The OECD member countries are: Australia, Austria, Belgium, Canada, Chile, the Czech Republic, Denmark, Estonia, Finland, France, Germany, Greece, Hungary, Iceland, Ireland, Israel, Italy, Japan, Korea, Luxembourg, Mexico, the Netherlands, New Zealand, Norway, Poland, Portugal, the Slovak Republic, Slovenia, Spain, Sweden, Switzerland, Turkey, the United Kingdom and the United States. The European Union takes part in the work of the OECD.

OECD Publishing disseminates widely the results of the Organisation's statistics gathering and research on economic, social and environmental issues, as well as the conventions, guidelines and standards agreed by its members.

OECD PUBLISHING, 2, rue André-Pascal, 75775 PARIS CEDEX 16
(23 2013 15 1 P) ISBN 978-92-64-19265-2 – No. 60529 2013-01